THE RACE

LAKELAND NIDHATAK

ISBN 979-8-88751-827-5 (paperback)
ISBN 979-8-88751-828-2 (digital)

Christian Faith Publishing
832 Park Avenue
Meadville, PA 16335
www.christianfaithpublishing.com

Printed in the United States of America

1

Only Dreamers Have Dreams
That Come True

The sun was up for an hour. Rays of light shone on the rock outcrops, melting away some of the last remnants of winter. The melted snow ran down over the sloping top of one of the rocks then down the side. When it reached the end of the suspended rock, it dripped several feet into a new puddle of water, steadily pounding the surface like a drum, yet silent. Off in the distance, at another rock outcrop, movement could be seen. The early morning spring silence was broken as a shout from the outcrop echoed through the valley, "Blessed be your name today, Lord God!" Then the sound of rhythmic pounding on the ground softly began as six runners bushwhacked through the woods.

A seventh runner, who was several minutes ahead of them, slipped off in the woods and hid, positioning himself to watch the others. Noticing an old campfire ring beside him, he picked up a burnt stick and rubbed it between his fingers. Then he took the black ash on his fingers and smeared it across both his cheeks and across his forehead. He lowered his body to the ground, watching and waiting until the last of the runners had gone by. Then he stood up, cupped his hands, and blasted out a coyote call that echoed through the woods. Then he began running after the group.

Knowing they were being chased, each one randomly took turns looking behind them. All the runners were sweating and breathing heavily, trying in vain to outrun their pursuer. The distance between the hunted and the hunter was eroding quickly. Then one by one, the hounded runners were passed by their pursuer. He came to a yellow metal gate, grabbed it with his hands, and flung his body over top. He ran over to his parked blue Jeep and stood up on the front brush guard. As the others began coming to the gate, he pulled out a baton under his shirt that was held around his neck with a blue nylon cord. On the baton was etched Hebrews 13:3. Using the baton as a makeshift microphone he announced, "I win! Lakeland Nidhatak is the first-place winner! Second place is my bestest friend Lawrence MacCabee. Third place is his beautiful sister Brisk MacCabee. Fourth place is my bestest brother Kenzie Nidhatak. Fifth place, a repeat weekend visitor from Thorndale Pennsylvania, is Kenzie's lovely girlfriend, Brandy Chugach. Sixth place, a first-time visitor also from Thorndale, Pennsylvania, is Brandy's brother, the rugged and talented Zachariah Chugach. And last but not least, the quietest person in the world, when he talks, people listen, the youngest of the MacCabee tribe, Parker MacCabee! And I repeat, the first-place winner in the First Annual Moonlight Overnight Crazy Man's Run, Lakeland Nidhatak! Applause to all!"

Everyone unenthusiastically clapped and said, "Yea!"

"You always win!" Lawrence said, laughing. "You know all the shortcuts!"

"I gave you five minutes lead time from the lookout, and I still caught you!" Lake replied.

"I about peed my pants when I heard that poor example of a coyote call," Zachariah said, laughing. "Then when I turned and saw you with that black stuff on your face, I almost peed them again! I think poor little Parker would have beaten everyone, but when he saw you with that stuff on your face, he laughed so hard he had to stop for a minute."

Parker, smiling widely, held up his hand and showed two fingers. "Oh, I stand corrected," Zachariah said. "He stopped for two minutes. Lake, did you ever come in first in a real race?"

"This is a real race," Lake replied as he jumped down from the brush guard. "If you meant an organized race, never. Probably never will. Usually the top 10 percent," Lake answered. There was a race in New York that every year I would end up tenth or twelfth. I always wondered why those ten or twelve wouldn't just stay home for just one year and let me win. The bastards."

"Did you run track in school?" Lawrence asked.

"Um, yeah, kind of. I went out for track in eighth grade, and I was beating some of the ninth graders in practice. Then I heard there would be a cut. They would get let go the ones they didn't think were good enough. So I felt I wasn't good enough and just dropped out to avoid the pain of the cut. I guess I didn't have much faith in myself back then. I would have survived the cut. I regret my decision."

"Here's some snacks everyone and some juice," Brisk told the runners as she placed the items on a large boulder by the gate.

"Why did you have faith in yourself back then?" Zachariah asked.

"Oh, I don't know. Let's get something to eat. Hey, did you have fun, Zachariah?" Lake asked.

"Yeah, it was fun. Thanks for asking Brandy to invite me up."

"Well, almost every weekend this spring, she comes up to visit Kenzie while they're out of school. When she said she has a brother who runs, I had to ask her to ask you to come up. So you had fun?"

"Yeah, it was great. Did you ever see on TV the first guy in the Boston Marathon being let by a police car? That could be you, Lake. It was so cool," Zachariah said while grabbing some snacks. "Thanks, Brisk."

"Well," Lake replied while filling up a cup with juice, "you know I don't watch TV, and I doubt I'll ever be in that position. My goal is to finish whatever race God has set before me, and to do it the best I can. That's what I want you all to set your minds on, finishing whatever dream God gives you and doing your best at it. Thanks for bringing the snacks today, Brisk. I always look forward to your homemade brownies and cookies. They're the bestest!"

"The best, you mean, Lakeland," Brandy said to correct Lake's vocabulary.

"That sure was a wonderful night," Brisk said to Lake. "I thought you were a little crazy asking us to run with you at midnight under a full moon, but it was absolutely beautiful!"

"Yes, it was! It was the bestest night," Lake answered, trying to agitate Brandy a little.

"I must admit, I liked being at the knoll, just talking about the Lord. And the singing and praying was super special too," Brandy said. "I guess I'll have to accept your misalignment of the English language if I want to enjoy your adventures."

Zachariah added, "I liked running down the grass roads under the moonlight. The leaves aren't out full yet, so once your night vision got adjusted, it was almost like daylight."

"How about that cold section with the snow in there yet?" Kenzie reminded them. "Looked like there were thousands of crystals in the snow reflecting the moonlight. It was so bright. We even had moon shadows!"

"And cold it was!" Zachariah said. "You're crazy, but you sure know how to have fun, Lake. Hey, you said Lakeland? I thought it was just Lake?"

"My full name is Lakeland Nidhatak. No middle name."

"Why'd they name you that?" Zachariah asked.

"Well, my folks were in the Northwest and Yukon Territories of Canada for twelve years. They built a cabin along a lake in the Yukon and named it Lakeland. That's where I was conceived."

"Your parents had sex? How gross!" Lawrence said, laughing. "I'm afraid to ask about Kenzie."

"Tell us about Kenzie," Zachariah asked.

"Well, you know his full name is Mackenzie Nidhatak. No middle name. When I was six, my family kayaked down the Mackenzie River and—"

"In the kayak?" Lawrence interrupted, still laughing. "That's disgusting!"

"No, no!" Lake said, also laughing. "He's named for the Mackenzie River because he was conceived along it, somewhere near Mackenzie Bay. I'm told it was a very cold night."

"Okay, enough of my parents' sex life. How's your car running?"

"Okay, change the subject, you mean," Lawrence said.

"Why'd your family move Mountain Springs? Why didn't you stay in Canada?" Zachariah asked him.

Lake looked at Kenzie and Kenzie shrugged his shoulders. "Well," Lake began, "I don't remember it well, but we had a big brother, Dawson. Yes, conceived in Dawson City in the Yukon. He drowned in the Yukon River when he was eleven. I was seven, and Kenzie was a baby. We moved here a few years later. They had relatives here in Mountain Springs. But my folks were never the same again. My mom would always cry, and my dad would always drink. Still does. A few years ago, just after our mom died, Kenzie and I flew up to Edmonton, Alberta, and then drove to Dawson City to find Dawson's grave. We didn't dare tell our dad, or he would have flipped out. We were there in July, and there was this awesome race up to the top of a mountain called the Dome overlooking Dawson City and the Yukon River. We both ran in it, and wow, it was so beautiful and wild going from the river to the Dome. No wonder they loved it there. It was a bittersweet adventure for both of us. Life is hard, but God is good, and the best is yet to come. So how's your car running?"

"Is that why you're so wild, Lake?" Zachariah asked.

"You can take the boy out of the wild, but you can't take the wild out of the boy," Lake responded.

"*Wild* sounds better than *crazy*," Brisk suggested.

"I think they're one in the same," Lawrence said with a smirk on his face.

"Thank you for those words of wisdom! Why do you think Kenzie is going to school to be a psychologist? He's going to use me for his senior project," Lake said, smiling while leaning up against his Jeep. "Let's go back to Base Camp and get cleaned up. Girls, use my cabin, no snooping please. And, guys, use the Eddy. I'll be fixing breakfast for you all at the Eddy this morning, compliments of the best Christian coffeehouse in Pennsylvania. Plus, during breakfast, I have a surprise proposal for all of you to consider. Let's pray before we leave. Father, thank you for another beautiful night. Thank you for allowing my friends to see your beauty in the night in the beautiful moonlight. Most people have never seen what we have witnessed.

Your creativity never ends. Thank you, in Jesus's name, amen. To the Eddy!"

"To the Eddy!" the rest repeated. Kenzie, Brandy, Lake, and Brisk left in the Jeep. Lawrence, Zachariah, and Parker followed in Lawrence's van.

Lake's cabin, which he calls Base Camp, and the Eddy were situated on twenty secluded rolling acres full of pine, spruce, and hemlock. Mountain laurel and rosebay rhododendrons filled in any openness. The Eddy was a multipurpose building. Christian musicians and speakers could assemble on the weekends and prayerfully experiment with their music or message. Lake thought up the name of the Eddy while on a kayak trip down Moshannon Creek. An eddy is calmer, somewhat protected area of water where one can pull in from the white water to relax before heading back out again. Lake wanted the Eddy to be a place where people can come and relax from the busyness of daily life.

On special nights, a dinner was prepared for guests, which would be followed with a time of communion, prayer, a short message, and then worship. Lake also used the building as a hostel and a bike rental business. It was of Lake's visions of the Eddy that inspired his friends to form the worship band the Judah Lions. They had occasionally played at schools, restaurants, and some bars, but Lake encouraged them to strictly play Christian music and honor God. Now they do the worship at church. Lawrence played the acoustic guitar while Zachariah played bass guitar. Brisk liked the recorder and the tambourine. Parker, who is autistic, was the most talented playing the keyboard, the saxophone, and practically any instrument he could get his hands on. Kenzie played the drums, and Brandy played the mandolin and the violin.

Arriving at the Eddy, the guys went in to get cleaned up, and the girls went to Lake's cabin to do the same. Lake sat outside while the others went in. After ten minutes had passed, Kenzie came back out and sat by his brother. "What are you thinking about, Lake?" he asked.

"I was just thanking God for a wonderful night," Lake answered. "I'm thrilled to have all my friends out there, and my brother too.

God's creativity never ends, and I just wanted you all to experience a full moon night like I do. To me, it's such a spiritual time—the bright moon, the stillness, the sounds of an awakening spring. God is so loving."

"Why are your eyes a little watery?" Kenzie asked.

"Oh, you know, um, when I sat down, I saw a flock of geese heading north," Lake replied.

"Lake, you are so sentimental. You are the one who always tells me that God is in control of our destinies. We are in this place and time according to his will. I wouldn't want to be anywhere else than here and now. Would you?"

"Do you think the gang had a good time?" Lake asked.

"Oh, they sure did. You should have come in and heard them. That's all they've been talking about since we got back. You're the 'adventure king,' Lake!"

"Really? They really had a good time?"

"Yes! They had a great time. Now get inside and get cleaned up because you told us you're making breakfast, remember?"

"Okay. I just want to be sure."

Kenzie looked at Lake then said, "You're the adventure king! We're hungry. I now give you the title of adventure cook too, so hurry up!" Lake smiled and patted his brother on the shoulder as they went inside.

Inside, Lawrence, Zachariah, and Parker were cleaned up. Lawrence and Zachariah were seated at a table, drinking orange juice while Parker was playing his keyboard. "Will you turn on the grill, Kenzie, while I grab a shower?" Lake asked.

"It's already on. We're hungry, remember?" Kenzie said with a smile.

"Give me two minutes, and I'll be out," Lake answered as he closed the door to the shower room.

"Kenzie," Lawrence called, "that was a fun night. We need to do something like that again."

"Yeah, that was so cool," Zachariah said. "I can't wait until it gets warmer, and we'd get out there again. I don't think I ever had so much fun."

"Well, maybe you need to tell that to Lake, okay? I think he'd be excited that you want to go back out. I had fun too. But I think you need to express it to him. I know he'd appreciate it."

After a few minutes, Lake came out of the shower room. He was wearing blue jeans and a blue flannel shirt. While rolling up his sleeves, he asked, "Hey, guys, how many of you want a cheese, egg, and sausage bagel sandwich?" Everyone raised a hand. Then Zachariah raised his other hand, and while laughing, everyone followed. "Okay, that's two sandwiches for everyone? I got it, you're hungry."

"Yes, hungry. That's spelled h-u-n-g-r-y," Kenzie said. "I'm getting my shower, and when I'm done, I'll need food! That's f-o-o-d. No energy bars for me!"

"Kenzie, what did the rabbit say to the dog?" Lake asked.

Kenzie said, "I don't know. What?"

"Bite me!" Lake answered with a smile. Everyone laughed, even Kenzie as he rolled his eyes and closed the shower room door.

"Those energy bars are pretty good," Lawrence said. "At least the first one or two, but after that, forget it. I couldn't eat any more. I need some real food."

"Lake, how far did we go?" Zachariah asked.

"About fourteen miles total. We ran the seven to the knoll. Then we were there for about two hours. We came back a different way, but it still was seven miles. So fourteen, that's my guesstimate," Lake replied while preparing breakfast.

Brandy and Brisk came in the Eddy. "Hey, guys, you all smell much better," Brisk said as she sniffed the air.

"I think it's my cooking that smells good, wouldn't you say?" Lake asked her.

"Lakeland, you have so many trophies and pictures in your study. Where'd you get all the trophies?" Brandy asked.

"Trophies to me are just a memory, nothing special about them. I don't boast about them. I boast in Christ alone. It's not how many trophies you've accumulated but how many trophies you've helped others acquire. Hey, I thought you and Brisk wouldn't snoop?" Lake asked while looking at Brisk smiling.

8

"Oh, Lake, we didn't snoop. I was just pointing out different pictures and items in your cabin. You should be proud of what you've have," she remarked.

"I'm joking. Snoop all you want. It's all God's blessings. He is so good me. He gave me the cabin, the Eddy, a future psychologist for a brother, and good musical running friends. Life is good!"

Kenzie came out of the shower room. He was wearing blue jeans and a tank top. Brandy walked over to him. Their embraced was followed by a long kiss.

Lake tapped the counter with his spatula. "Excuse me, kids," he said, laughing. "This is a Christian establishment."

Kenzie momentarily broke the kiss to say, "That's good because we're Christians," then continued to kiss Brandy.

"Do you kiss like that, Lake?" Brisk asked.

"Yes, I do, but you couldn't handle it," Lake replied.

Brisk started to laugh then Lawrence, Zachariah, and Parker joined in.

Lake looked at them and shook his head. Then he placed his hands on the counter and flipped his body over it. He grabbed Brisk, leaned her back onto his arms, and kissed her.

The guys applauded. Brisk said, "You do know how to kiss."

As Lake walked behind the counter, he said, "I'm the adventure king, the adventure cook, now the adventure kisser. I think that's a triathlon. Those Nidhatak boys are animals!"

Kenzie and Brandy went to sit down with the others as Lake continued making breakfast. When Kenzie sat down, he started singing, "H-u-n-g-r-y, h-u-n-g-r-y." Then everyone joined in, "H-u-n-g-r-y, h-u-n-g-r-y, h-u-n-g-r-y." They didn't stop until each one had a breakfast sandwich in front of them.

"Thank you, boys and girls, for teaching me how to spell *hungry*," Lake said. "Seriously now, will you pray, Lawrence?" he asked.

"Why don't you pray?" Lawrence responded.

"Okay, I'll pray," Lake told him. "This is how you do it, Lawrence: Father, you are so good, so great. Thank you again for a beautiful night and a beautiful morning. Thank you for these brothers and sisters gathered here. Thank you for this food. In Jesus's name, amen."

"See, Lawrence, just say plainly what is in your heart. Praise God for what he has done. Then close in Jesus's name."

Lawrence replied, "Then why in church is it so long and with those big words no one understands?"

"Well, people pray differently," Lake answered. "Some think they have to impress God. Some think they have to impress anyone listening. God simply wants to know your heart. He knows what you are going to ask before you ask him. How can you impress God?"

"You can't," Zachariah told them.

"Exactly," Lake said.

"What proposal did you want to ask us?" Lawrence asked.

"I was wondering if anyone remembered me saying that," Lake said as he walked over to the white bulletin board. He erased all the messages and started writing. Brisk read along as Lake was writing. "The…100…Mile…Northern…Tier…Ultra…and…Relay…Race. The 100 Mile Northern Tier Ultra and Relay Race. What are you up to, Lake?"

"Let me describe the race, then I'll take your questions. First, you all did about fourteen miles last night, and you all look good. I planned that to see how well you'd do before I actually mentioned this race to you. Anyway, I thought we could run this as a relay team under your band's name, the 'Judah Lions.' Everyone would have to run twice. There would be about an hour or two break between each of your runs. The distances vary, but one hundred divided by six would be approximately 16.6 miles a piece, so basically, each runner would have roughly two eight-mile sections. I think you could do it in under twenty hours.

"I thought on the front of your T-shirts you could put 'Judah Lions' and on the back something like 'Parker, keyboard' or 'Mackenzie, lead drummer' or 'Zachariah, bass guitar.' That could start up a conversation with another runner about your Christian walk or run in this case. I decided against slogans like 'turn or burn' or even something hip like 'Yo, Jesus is coming back and he's going to kick yo ass.' What do you think about the whole idea?"

"I like the 'Yo' one," Zachariah said, laughing.

"I wish we could figure out how you brain works, Lake," Lawrence interjected. "You have some weird ideas in there."

"I think we could do it," Kenzie told the group with a serious look on his face. "I think we should attempt it."

"What, figure out how Lake's brain works?" Zachariah asked.

"No! The race! No one can possibly figure out how his brain works," Kenzie said. "How long until the race, Lake?"

"Four months," Lake replied. "What's wrong with how my brain works?"

"I vote for the doing the race," Kenzie said while raising his right hand. Parker put his hand up.

"That's two," Kenzie added.

"I'm in," Brandy said, raising her hand.

"So am I!" Zachariah yelled, raising his hand.

"Count me in. I love a challenge," Brisk told them, raising her hand.

"I guess you need a lead guitar for this, or it wouldn't be the whole band," Lawrence said, looking at the others. "Okay, I'm in."

Everyone shouted as Lawrence raised his right hand and all joined their hands with his.

They began chanting, "Judah Lions, Judah Lions, Judah Lions."

Then Kenzie said, "Wait a minute. You said six runners. What are you going to run Lake?"

"It's an ultra. The whole thing," Lake replied.

"Lake, that's too far. Way too far. You tried it last year and didn't make it. You said you'd never run an ultra again."

"I always say that."

"You're getting old, you're almost twenty-nine. You need to watch yourself," Kenzie said.

"I made it seventy-six miles last year, you know that. What's twenty-four miles more? Besides, the best age for ultra-runners is thirty to fifty."

"Lake!" Kenzie yelled.

"Kenzie!" Lake replied, yelling louder.

"Why not do a 100K instead of 100 miles?"

"A 100K? I do those for practice!"

"Did you tell dad about this?" Kenzie asked.

"Yup."

"What did he say?"

"That I was an idiot. What did you expect?"

"I'm not sure I can dispute that!"

"Well, thank you for your vote of confidence!"

"Look," Kenzie began. "You don't need to prove you can do this to anyone. Just be my normal brother. Run with us. Can't you just be normal?"

"No, I can't. Plus, I'm not trying to prove anything. I just want to do this. I need to do this. I need to try again. Last year was the only race I didn't finish. Besides, it's too late. We're already signed up," Lake said with a smile.

"You crazy bastard," Kenzie said, laughing and shaking his head.

"Dream big, little bro. Only dreamers have dreams that come true. Life is short. God is good, and the best is yet to come," Lake told Kenzie. "Dream! Run! Endure! Celebrate!"

"Wow, Lake," Lawrence said. "You have a lot of faith in us, don't you?"

"Yes, I do. I'll help in any way I can. I'll be your coach and your spiritual leader," Lake told them. "We have four months until the race."

"Hey, everybody," Brandy whispered. "Look at Parker on the keyboard." Everyone turned and looked toward Parker. He was fast asleep with his head rested on the keyboard.

"We all better get some sleep too. It's three hours until church," Lake told them.

"I can't wait until we play at worship today. After last night, I just want to praise the Lord. It was such a beautiful night," Brisk said. "Lawrence, help me get our little brother to a bunk."

The guys settled down into the men's bunkroom, and the girls went into the women's bunkroom.

Lake went outside and got into his hammock on the porch. After a while Kenzie came out.

"Lake, why are you out here?" Kenzie asked.

"It's too dark in the bunkroom. The sleep problem. I don't want to have one of those nightmares while everyone is here. Besides, I can watch the geese fly north out here."

"Is there anything I can do for you?" Kenzie asked.

"Well, I bet you have a sleeping bag in your hand in case I ask you to sleep out here on the porch."

"You always know what I'm thinking!" Kenzie said as he threw his sleeping bag down on the porch. "Why'd I bother asking?"

"Look at that sun, little bro." Lake pointed out to the eastern horizon. "God is planning another beautiful spring day. Can't wait to be in church today to just sing and sing."

"It is beautiful. You're right, Lake, his creativity never ceases."

Lake prayed, "Thank you, Father, for what is before our eyes. Protect my brother Kenzie. Use him mightily for you. Bless all our friends inside. Use them mightily for you. Thank you for everything that transpired since the sun went down. It was an awesome night. In Jesus's name, amen." As he looked down from the hammock at Kenzie on the porch floor, he said, "Have a good nap, little bro, I love you." Kenzie was already asleep. Lake rolled back, looking toward the sky. Another flock of geese headed north. With tears in his eyes, he closed them and shortly fell asleep.

2

Growing Pains

Church was over, and people were leaving the South Brook Christian Center. The Judah Lions Band, which were members of the church worship team, were stepping off the podium, and Lake met them at the door. "You guys were awesome today!" he said.

"That's because of the wonderful adventure you took us on last night!" Brisk replied.

"I just kept thinking on how beautiful the moon and stars were last night. I didn't want to stop praising him," Kenzie said.

"I'm tired," Lawrence whined.

"We're tired, but no one is too tired for our usual after church ice cream, right?" Brandy asked.

"Ice cream!" Zachariah exclaimed.

"Then a run," Lake teased.

"No!" the others replied.

"All right," Lake said with a big smile. "I know your limits."

"Wait, guys. My folks are expecting us for an Easter brunch, remember? Can you all make it? I know you're all tired," Brisk asked.

"When?" Zachariah asked.

"As soon as we are all sitting down at the table," she replied.

"My mom sure can cook a good home meal, Zack," Lawrence added.

"Sounds good to me," Lake told them. "Sure hope your dad took a 'nice' pill today."

"Lake, my dad is nice. He is just a little rough around the edges," Brisk replied.

"He sure must have a lot of 'edges'! He's my dad's friend, and like my dad, he likes to agitate me."

"He won't bother you," she assured him.

"Last time I was there, he was as friendly as a pissed off rattlesnake," Lake remarked.

"Well, he was sleeping, and you cranked up Parker's electric guitar," Lawrence said, laughing hysterically. "That was hilarious—him chasing you out of the house!"

"Oh, it was a riot. Are you sure I'm invited?" Lake asked.

"Lakeland Nidhatak," Pastor Bentley called to the group.

"Yes, sir," Lake answered.

"I'd like to see you in the adult Sunday schoolroom please."

"Sure. Will it be long?"

"No. Not at all."

"I'll be right back," Lake told the gang. "Meet you in the parking lot."

In the adult Sunday schoolroom sat several members of the Sunday school class. Pastor Bentley and Lake went in and sat down.

"Lake," Pastor Bentley began, "several Sundays ago, you asked the class to write their own song or psalm for Sunday school, is that correct?"

"Yes, sir. We were discussing 'singing a new song to the Lord,' and I mentioned we all should make an attempt to write our own song or psalm. Of course, you were having coffee and doughnuts and usually don't attend Sunday school yourself so someone else in this room must have tattled on me, correct?"

Pastor Bentley sighed then continued, "And that would have been due last Sunday, correct?"

"Yes, your honor."

"No need to get smart, Lakeland. I'm told you also made a smart comment to those who did not fulfill your assignment."

"I think I made a correct assessment."

"Lakeland, calling your fellow brothers and sisters 'stinking, lazy-ass Christians' is uncalled for...especially in church!"

"Even if it's an accurate statement?"

"Lakeland Nidhatak, that is not appropriate behavior in my church—"

"It's not your church," Lake interrupted. "It's Jesus's church. And what's not appropriate in telling the truth? What is so difficult about writing a praise to God? Aren't these Christian people and isn't praising God a daily Christian function?"

"Lakeland, some people don't have the time, or it may be a personal thing."

"Male cow feces! They just didn't bother. That's all. Christianity is not a spectator sport!"

"Well, they request, and I support, banning you from Sunday school for the rest of the year. They also request an apology."

"An apology? For stating the truth? Well, of course!" Lake turned and faced the other church members. "Okay, okay. I asked a simple thing and you couldn't even do it in a week's time. That would be seven days, or 168 hours, or 10,080 minutes, or 604,800 seconds. Apologize? All right, here goes: I'm truly sorry I call you all 'stinking, lazy ass Christians.' None of you stink. I'm sorry."

"Nidhatak!" Pastor Bentley yelled.

"Wake up and check the hour!" Lake shouted as he left the room.

Just down the hall, someone grabbed Lake's arm and pulled him into an empty classroom. It was the pastor's son, Justin. "Don't you talk to my father like that, Nid-has-been!"

"It's Nidhatak, Justin. Your dad and I were having a discussion, and as usual, he is right…kind of."

"When I am in charge here one day, you and your little merry band will be out on the street. I'll be running my church the way I see fit."

"It's Jesus's church."

"Shut up, you dirtbag. And by the way, remember that silly running mini sermon you gave during open Sunday about how runners in a race accelerate as they approach the finish line?"

"Right. The point was as we get older, we should accelerate as Christians, as we near our finish line."

"Well, that was stupid. And I want you to understand that the applause had nothing to do with you!"

"But the congregation really enjoyed what I said. You never get an applause because you are kind of snooty and cold," Lake said with a smile, trying to add humor to the conversation.

"It had nothing to do with you! Do you understand?"

"Maybe they were applauding God?"

"Shut up and get out of my church!"

"It's not—"

"Shut up!"

"Fine, Justin. Have a good day."

"If I were you, Nid-has-been, I'd watch my back. In my book, you are a marked man."

Lake went out to the parking lot and began to get in his Jeep. Brisk rushed over and asked, "Everything okay, Lake?"

"Oh, yeah. Bentley is pissed at me…again. It's always something. If it's not one thing it's another. Let's get out of Dodge."

Everyone was seated at the MacCabee dinner table. Mr. MacCabee said grace, and the dinner was served. "Everything looks and smells great, Mom," Brisk told her.

"Yes, Mrs. MacCabee, everything looks and smells great," Lake added.

As usual at dinner, Mr. MacCabee, a firm and serious man, asked a question to his guests to commence a healthy discussion. He asked, "Was Jesus rich?"

"No," said Lawrence.

"I'd says 'yes,'" Lake responded.

"This should be a good discussion," Mr. MacCabee suggested.

"Well," Lawrence began, "he had to get a coin from a fish to pay taxes, so he must have been poor."

"Some guy must have dropped his wallet into the water for the fish to get the coin," Zachariah said.

"How did the fish get into the wallet to get the coin?" Mr. MacCabee asked.

"They did not have wallets back then. They had purses," Brandy pointed out.

"How did the fish get into the purse to get the coin?" Mr. MacCabee asked.

"Maybe there was no purse. Perhaps a Roman soldier threw someone into the water and left him to drown," Brisk wondered.

"How did the fish get into the person's clothes to get the coin?" Mr. MacCabee asked, thoroughly enjoying the conversation.

"Maybe someone made a wish and tossed the coin into the water," Lawrence suggested. "But however the fish got the coin, Jesus needed it to pay the tax, so he was poor."

"Why do you think he was rich, Lakeland?" Mr. MacCabee asked.

"Well, his father owns everything, right? The cattle on a thousand hills. He gave all up to invade Earth, and he lived a poor life but he had an inheritance waiting for him, just as we do. So no matter how poor he or we are here on earth because of our inheritance, he and we are rich. Also, how the fish got the coin, I think, somewhat respectfully, is a very elementary conversation question especially since it is Easter."

Mr. MacCabee stared at Lake. Lake nervously wondered what Mr. MacCabee was thinking and what his response would be.

"Kenzie, why do you have a black door on your red Jeep?" Brisk asked, sensing the tenseness between Lake and her father.

As he started to smile knowing Brisk was trying to change the subject, Kenzie replied, "Because some unnamed person didn't know how to use their mirrors before they backed up."

"Well, no one is supposed to park in the backup area. It's for backing up," Lake replied.

"Hey, everyone. What did Lake say when he got out of his Jeep after backing into me?" Kenzie teased.

The group responded in unison, "It's always something. If it's not one thing it's another." Then everyone laughed.

"Parker told me you got a BMW, Lakeland. Is that true?" Mr. MacCabee asked.

"Well, when we run, we joke about getting a BMW," Lake explained. "BMW stands for bloody, muddy, and wet. That's what Parker was referring to."

"I haven't seen your father lately. You know he's a good friend of mine. How is he, Lakeland?" Mr. MacCabee asked.

"Ah, okay, I guess," Lake answered.

"What do you mean *you guess*?" Mr. MacCabee snipped at Lake.

"Oh, the pill is wearing off. Well, I don't know how he is. I haven't seen him."

"Comments you make in front of Parker and Lawrence, is there more that we should know?"

"Ah, no," Lake responded.

"We'll talk later."

"Ah, no, we won't."

"Don't tell me what we won't discuss in my house!" Mr. MacCabee angrily told Lake.

"I didn't mean any disrespect. I just don't want to discuss that subject."

"Let me tell you what we will discuss: you getting my children to go to that rock and roll, chandelier-swinging thing you call church! What is it? South Brook Christian Center?"

"South Brook, that's the name."

"You got them playing guitars and all kinds of hippie crap!"

"They play worship music wonderfully. You should come hear them some time."

"I wouldn't step foot in there. You call that a church?"

"Daddy, please stop," Brisk pleaded.

"This must be 'Pick on Lake' Day," Lake mused.

"Don't be a wise punk in my house!" Mr. MacCabee said, red-faced with anger.

"Punk!" Lake said as he stood up. "That's my cue word! Thank you, Mrs. MacCabee, for a wonderful Easter brunch. And, Mr. MacCabee, I can't wait until I am old so I can be as nasty and miserable as you and my dad are. Good day!"

Back at the cabin, Lake was working down by the creek on one of his mountain-bike trails. Sheba was standing in the water, barking at Lake. She wanted him to throw the ball so she could chase it once again. Each time she'd retrieve the ball and returned, she'd drop it in the water and bark at Lake to get the ball and throw it again.

Before Lake could pick up the ball as it floated downstream, Sheba ears went up, and she ran up the trail, barking. She quickly returned, frantically wagging her tail as she ran toward Lake. This was her way of announcing friendly company. It was Kenzie.

"Hey," Lake said, acknowledging Kenzie's presence, knowing he was about to get scolded by his phycology major little brother.

"What's your problem, Lake?" Kenzie began.

"Nothing. Where's Brandy?"

"She's up at the cabin, and she's not the subject of this conversation."

Lake threw his shovel into the creek. "Okay. It's your turn. Tell me how wrong I was about something, tell me how stupid I am, tell me how rude I am—"

"You did nothing wrong, and you aren't stupid. You were rude, though."

"I hate that 'punk' word."

"Lake. You've hurt practically everyone's feelings. Didn't we have an awesome night last night? Didn't we have a good church service? Seems you get one little verbal arrow shot by someone and you go into survival mode. Someone hurts your feelings, and you never want anything to do with them ever again."

"You can thank your father for all that," Lake responded as he retrieved his shovel.

"He's your father too, Lake," Kenzie said with a little sympathy. "You should call Mrs. MacCabee and apologize. Right? Right, Lake?" Lake kept digging and didn't reply. "Oh, so now you are going into the silent mode. Fine, I'm leaving. Goodbye!" Kenzie turned and began walking up the trail. "I'm leaving, Lake! Goodbye!"

Lake waved goodbye then threw a rock into the creek for Sheba to find. Then he kept on digging.

"You're one stubborn bastard, mud-face boy," Kenzie yelled while returning to the creek.

"I knew you wouldn't leave," Lake replied. "You always have to finish your objective no matter how wrong it is."

"It's not wrong that I care about our friends and care about you, mud butt."

"Why does everyone get mad at me? Why does it seem everything I do is wrong? I mean Bentley is mad, old man MacCabee is mad, Pete is mad, God is mad—"

"Pete from church? Pete's Petrol Palace?"

"Precisely. Pete's Petrol Palace is permanently peed at poor, pitiful me."

"What did you do to Pete, Lake?"

"Oh, I guess I pulled too close to the pumps and bumped a hose off and I ran over it. No damage, just a little gas on the pavement. Pete ran out screaming at me! I was morbidly embarrassed!"

"What did you do then, Lake?"

"Um, I got my lighter out and pretended I was going to light it. He backed off real quick!" Kenzie closed his eyes and shook his head.

"Well, I now know why Pete is mad as well as Mr. MacCabee. Why is Bentley mad? What did you do to him, Lake?"

"Oh, you just never mind, psycho boy."

"Psychology boy would be more accurate, mud man. What happened with Bentley?"

"All right! In our class, I kind of gave an assignment for everyone to write their own song or psalm and only two did it. I casually may have called them stinking, lazy-ass Christians. Someone told on me, and now Bentley banned me from class. Wish I was banned from church so I wouldn't have to endure his sermons."

"Lake, he does good sermons."

"Yeah, right. He should be like John Allen at his Bible study. He so loves the Lord and so good at teaching. He should be the pastor. Bentley is as good at sermons as I am at making friends at the gas station."

"It sounds like you are back to normal now, making jokes."

"I'm always normal."

"No comment."

"Hey, that's not nice. You're supposed to be my brother!"

"Seriously, Lake. You've got to stop allowing these comments, these verbal arrows from wounding you. We both are wounded by dad, you more than me. At the MacCabees', all would have been well if you would have avoid reacting to that one word."

21

"I hate that word! Dad always used it against his own sons," Lake said with tears.

"I know. I know. Listen, as for the situation at church, maybe, if you just accept that people, for whatever reason, did not write a psalm on your time schedule." Lake rolled his eyes. "And Pete's Petrol Palace," Kenzie continued, "an abrupt sincere apology may have smoothed things over and avoided any hostilities. Please go back and apologize."

"To whom?

"Everybody!"

"I don't think so. I mean, I would, but they would think I was weak and they won."

"Lake! It's not about you! What would Jesus have done?"

"He would have called Bentley a pharisee, told MacCabee 'get behind me, Satan,' and sent a lightning bolt down on Pete's Petrol Palace."

"Lake, I know you don't really think that. I think the Lord is dealing with you to humble yourself to apologize and to forgive."

"I'll think about it, Kenzie. You know I always do try to make things right. Right now, I'd rather just avoid any hostile humanoids for a while. I just don't understand while it is so difficult to get along with people, especially Christians."

"Lake, it takes two to create a conflict. It takes two to sign a peace treaty."

"I know. Remember I told you that, Mr. Plagiarist. Let's go up to the cabin. I'm hungry. I didn't have much lunch, remember that too?"

"That's your fault. Hey, muddy Lake, I think I also heard you say God was mad at you too. What's it this time?"

"Well," Lake began as the brothers began walking up the trail. "I was coming home and stopped along a dirt road to take a leak. I walked down over the embankment. As I was taking care of business, I heard a loud bang. I thought it was a gunshot. I quickly ran up the bank, but no one was around. Then I looked at the Jeep. A dead tree fell right across it!"

"No way!" Kenzie said as he began laughing.

"For real, Kenzie! What are the chances you stop to pee and a tree falls on your vehicle!"

Kenzie, laughing hysterically, barely was able to respond, "I bet you were pissed! No pun intended! Or maybe it was!"

"I was livid! I was like, God, are you really that mad at me? I couldn't believe it. It put a big dent right across the roof line."

"Well, pee, boy," Kenzie said, still laughing. "I don't think God is mad at you, but he certainly is trying to get your attention."

"Well, he did! I wish he had done it in a less damaging and embarrassing way. How do I explain that to the insurance company?"

"I would not mention why you stopped along the road. That maybe too much information. Bet they would laugh if you did! Sorry, but that's hilarious. Okay. What are you going to do after you eat?"

"Apologization."

"That's not a word."

"I'm going to call or visit and attempt apologization."

"*Apologization* is not a word."

"Yes, Kenzie. It is a word. I saw it as the word for today in the newspaper. I finally know something you don't know."

"Well, congratulations. Anyway, making things right sounds like the brother I know. Hey, when we get to the cabin can you watch my Jeep for a minute?"

"What for?"

"I have to pee!"

"You!" Lake began chasing Kenzie. "You're going to wear the mud on this shovel! Get him, Sheba!"

"Brandy! Help!"

3

Trouble Brewing: Sheep vs. Wolves

The following Sunday, after leading worship at South Brook Christian Center, the band settled in next to where Lake was sitting. A large man dressed in white was seated up front next to the church's minister, Pastor Bentley. Lawrence whispered to Lake, "Who is the dude in white?" Lake responded by shrugging his shoulders. "He looks like that dude in those old *Dukes of Hazard* TV shows," Lawrence said with a big smile.

"Who?" Zachariah asked.

"Boss Hogg," Lawrence answered then started laughing. The group started laughing until Pastor Bentley glared at them.

Lake didn't laugh but whispered to Brisk, "I don't know who he is, but I have a bad feeling in my spirit about him. Something's just not right."

Pastor Bentley stood to address the congregation: "As many of you know, I'll be away several weeks on vacation. It was hard to find a pastor willing to fill in for me, but we've located someone highly recommended and one that I'm sure will be able to handle the needs here at South Brook. Please welcome Pastor Chase Avalon, president of Chase Avalon Ministries." Pastor Avalon stood as the congregation gave him a welcome applause. "Pastor Avalon will pray for the offering and will be followed by Lakeland Nidhatak's short message about the persecuted church. Then Pastor Avalon will be bringing today's message.

"What message are you giving, Lake?" Brisk asked.

Lake replied, "I mentioned to Pastor Bentley that we need to be praying for the persecuted church, and he said we would. I don't want to go up there."

"You better think fast, Lake," Lawrence said while laughing.

"I better pray fast," Lake said.

Pastor Avalon began to pray for the offering. "Glorious, gracious heavenly Trinity, with holy humbleness we submit freely to you our earthly wealth for your 'nurturation' of your local body today. Steadfastly we beg of Thee to accept our meager offering to the greatness of your precious love contrary to this unworthy congregation."

Lawrence whispered, "Press 1 for English, 2 for Spanish, and 3 for I don't know what the hell he said." Parker and Zachariah started laughing. Brisk looked at them and went, "Shhhhhh."

Pastor Bentley responded to the prayer, "Hmmm, that's a prayer! Okay, Lakeland, will you come forward now?"

"How'd I get myself in to this?" Lake murmured as he slid through the pew to the aisle.

Lake was extremely nervous behind the microphone and wouldn't look at the congregation. After thirty quiet seconds, he smiled and said, "Repeat after me: Blessed be your name today, Lord God!"

The congregation loudly responded, "Blessed be your name today, Lord God!"

With that, Lake began his presentation with a little more confidence. "Ah, I had asked Pastor Bentley if we could regularly pray for the persecuted church around the world. Christians, who are our brothers and sisters, are being tortured and even killed every hour because of their faith in Jesus. We need to be remembering them and praying for them."

"The baton," Lawrence whispered with cupped hands aimed toward Lake.

"Oh, the baton." Lake pulled a baton from under his shirt. "I carry this baton to remember to pray for the persecuted church. Etched on it is Hebrews 13:3, 'Remember those in bonds as if in bonds with them.' The baton also symbolizes to me that with each

Christian's death, they pass the baton of the Gospel on to the next generation. Even you, someday, will pass your baton onto a member of your family, or to a friend or—"

Pastor Avalon interrupted Lake. "Let me tell you about persecution. I have suffered for the cause. People have called me names, scratched my car, and even left the church because of my godly preaching. I have suffered, let me tell you."

Lake responded, "Sir, I'm talking about real suffering, not superficial. Our brothers and sisters are beaten and—"

"Please be seated," Pastor Avalon told Lake. "What could you possibly know about the persecuted church?"

Lake looked at Pastor Bentley, who then signaled him to sit down. Before he did, Lake walked over to Pastor Bentley and whispered, "Something is not right with this guy. My spirit was grieved before I even came up here."

"Don't be silly, Lake. Just be quiet and sit down, it must be something you ate."

Lake walked off the podium and sat down. Kenzie patted him on the shoulder and said, "Good job, big bro." But Lake felt he had failed and that Pastor Avalon stole the show.

Pastor Avalon spoke for one hour and twenty minutes, mostly about himself. Many people were politely leaving the service to escape the soulish message. Lake held his head in his hands. Parker and Zachariah were asleep.

When the church service was finally over, most of the congregation left immediately. The band remained in their seats, talking together. Pastors Bentley and Avalon walked over to them. "Everyone," Pastor Bentley began, "you all did a fine job being the lead worshippers today. Ah, I'll be gone starting next week, and Pastor Avalon would like you to do just two or three songs instead of the usual five or six. He wants to sing some old hymns and a solo or two by himself. Would that be all right?"

"Sure, I guess," Lawrence answered.

"We can do hymns," Kenzie reminded them, but Pastor Avalon shook his head no.

"No, Pastor Avalon will handle the hymns."

"When will you be back?" Kenzie asked.

"Four or five weeks," Pastor Bentley answered.

"That long?" Lawrence asked.

"That's not a problem, Lawrence, is it?" Pastor Bentley asked.

"Don't scatter your sheep," Lake said to Pastor Bentley.

"What on Earth are you talking about, Lake?"

"When the shepherd is away, the wolves will play," Lake said. Then he turned and left the church. The band followed.

Pastor Bentley turned and headed toward his office with Pastor Avalon beside him. "Hmmm, don't scatter your sheep. Wonder what he was talking about. Oh well, he always was a little weird."

"I've dealt with hillbillies before," Pastor Avalon answered. "He probably doesn't know much beyond these mountains. Just a novice, stupid boy."

"Pastor Avalon, I'm surprised at that statement," Pastor Bentley said.

"I only speak truth," Pastor Avalon responded.

"Well, okay, I guess," Pastor Bentley said as he gave in. "Well, my wife said dinner will be ready shortly, so we better head over to the parsonage."

"Great," Pastor Avalon said, "I'm hungry."

Outside, Brisk asked, "Lake, what do you mean about the sheep comment?"

"I think this guy is going to disrupt this church body," he told her. "People are going to leave. I think he's a wolf in sheep's clothing."

"Do you really think that?" Brisk asked very seriously.

"I don't think it. I know it," he told her.

"What should we do?" Brandy asked.

"We are, quote, unquote, lower-level Christians so no one, not even Bentley, will listen to us. We don't belong to the upper-level social club. But we do have a weapon," Lake told the group.

"What's that?" Lawrence asked.

"Prayer. We will pray that, if I'm right, God will intervene. If I'm wrong, we will pray that God corrects me."

"What do you mean by 'lower-level Christians?" Zachariah asked.

"Well, one time Kenzie and I asked if the church would consider an evening service on Sunday night. We were told the church wouldn't because the 'upper level' Christians wouldn't come. So we concluded we must be the lower-level Christians."

Kenzie added, "But we couldn't help wondering if the 'upper-level' Christians won't come to any service except Sunday mornings, how can they be 'upper-level' Christians?"

"Must be money and worldly status?" Zachariah asked.

"And Bingo was his name," Lake answered. "That's why we have a Sunday night service at the Eddy. Just us 'lower levels.'"

"Hi, Lakeland. Hi, Mackenzie. Hi boys and girls," an aristocratic-looking woman said as she approached the group.

"Speaking of upper levels," Lake whispered. "Hi, Mrs. Mahoosic. I see you got another new Cadillac."

"Oh, yes," she said proudly. "I didn't like the color of last year's model, so I got a new one."

"How are things on the mission board going?" Lake deliberately asked.

"Not well," Mrs. Mahoosic told him. "Not many people giving to missions. Only a few dollars here and there. I can't give much myself because I have my new car and my condo at Myrtle Beach. Plus, the dues at the country club are outrageous. Come to think of it, the only ones who give are the poorer people in the church, like yourselves."

"Us lower-level Christians?" Kenzie asked.

"Exactly," she said. "You might as well keep it because it doesn't amount to much."

"Well, it doesn't amount to much to you, but I know Jesus multiplies it," Lake told her.

"Whatever little fantasy you want to believe," she replied. "Oh, you Nidhatak boys are so cute and gullible. That reminds me, I heard your father has another girlfriend. Is that true?"

"You tell me, you usually do," Lake replied. "Come to think of it, he changes girlfriends as much as you change Cadillacs."

"Lakeland, I think you're right," she said. "So he should be good for another year."

"And so should you! That's so amazing!" Lake sarcastically told her.

"Well, got to go play some golf with the county commissioners. Bye-bye, boys and girls," she said as she walked to her car.

"Goodbye, Mrs. Mahoosic," Lake replied.

"Lakeland, that's not funny. You shouldn't egg her on like that," Brandy told him.

"I was just playing her game. I don't think it was funny either, not funny at all. Actually, kind of sad, very sad," he said as he watched Mrs. Mahoosic drive away. "Christians!" he said with disgust.

"Are we going to Michael and Susan's Ice Cream Parlor as usual?" Lawrence asked. "I'm hungry, and it's hot."

"Let go," Lake said. The group walked a few buildings down the street from the church and went into an ice cream shop. They sat together at one large table and made their orders.

"Will you pray, Lawrence?" Lake asked.

"Why don't you pray, Lake?" he responded.

"All right. Father, thank you for another beautiful day. We pray for discernment regarding the things at church today. We want only what you want. Give us guidance on what we should do if we should do anything at all. Thank you for the ice cream. In Jesus's name. Amen."

While everyone was talking and eating their ice cream two ladies walked over to the group. "Hi there. How are you all?" one said.

Lake stood up and said, "We're all fine. How are you?"

"Very good," she said. "We saw you praying. Are you Christians?"

"Yes," Lake told her. "This is Brisk, Kenzie, Brandy, Lawrence, Zachariah, and Parker. I'm Lake. We're all children of the King."

"Here's our ministry card, if you care to contact us," one woman said.

"Well, thank you," Lake said. "Would you like to join us?"

"It depends, do you sin?" the other woman asked.

"What?" Lake asked surprised.

"Do you sin?" she asked again.

"Sin?" he asked again.

"Yes, *sin*. Do you sin?" she asked.

"Ah, yes. We are all sinners," Lake answered.

"Then you're not Christians. James makes it clear that if you sin, you are not Christians," the other woman sternly told them.

"You don't sin? Not at all?" Lawrence asked.

"No. We don't sin. We are perfect," one woman replied.

Brisk reached for Lake's hand, knowing he was getting upset with the way the conversation was going.

"Perfect?" he asked. "There was only one perfect man and we all killed him," Lake told them.

"The Romans and the Jews killed him," she replied.

"Do you always stop fully at a stop sign?" Lake asked her.

"What do you mean?" she asked.

"Every time you come to a stop sign, do you come to a complete stop?" he asked again.

"Of course not, no one does," she angrily replied.

"Well, the law says you are to come to a complete stop. That's the law. If you are breaking the law, then you are sinning," he told her.

"Driving is different. It doesn't count," she said.

"Would Jesus break the law?" Lake asked.

"No, of course not," she replied.

"If he was here and pulled up to a stop sign in his Jeep, I'm sure he'd drive a Jeep, would he run the stop sign?" he asked.

"He wouldn't. This is a stupid conversation," she told him.

"There, he would not because it would be a sin, and he can't sin, but you do, we all do. There is none perfect except him," Lake firmly told them.

"You need to read your Bible. You know nothing. We are perfect. Enjoy hell!" she said as the two women stormed out.

Lake sat down and started eating his ice cream. No one spoke. Then Lake bolted outside to the women as they were getting in their car. The others remained inside, watching.

"He sure has more guts than I do," Lawrence said. "Look, he's coming back in!"

Lake came in, sat down, and began eating his ice cream.

A few minutes later, the women came back in. Lake kept eating. "Okay, everyone, your 'leader' said we need to apologize, or he won't give us our keys back. You know, we could call the police."

"Go ahead," Lake told them. "And I'll call the newspaper and tell them what happened and give them this ministry card. 'Loving Sisters in Christ Ministries.' Wow, your love is overwhelming here this Sunday afternoon. Is it the same the rest of the week, I mean, are you more perfect any specific day, or is it all the same?"

"We apologize for your misunderstanding of biblical truth," one woman said.

Lake stood up and faced her up close. "We probably do have some misunderstandings of biblical truth because we aren't perfect. Let me ask you, if you were indeed 'Loving Sisters in Christ,' where was your love when you told us to 'enjoy hell'? Seriously, is that love?"

"Please, we must be going, we have a conference to attend. We apologize."

"What's the name of the conference? What's the name of the conference!" Lake demanded.

"How to love your brothers and sisters more. Are you happy?"

"It depends. Who are the speakers?"

"We are," one said, looking slightly ashamed.

"Then I'm very sad... I'm grieved actually. The keys are on top of your car."

Without saying anything further, the women went out and got in their car. As they drove away, one of the women gave the group her middle finger.

"I can't believe she did that," Brisk said.

"Christians," Lake replied. "If it wasn't for Christians, there'd be more Christians."

"What?" Zachariah asked.

"Think about it," Lawrence told him.

Then, while eating, Lake prayed, "Father, I'm not sure of the purpose of that conversation, but we pray for their eyes to be open to the full truth. I will not judge their salvation. I ask that you move their hearts closer to your heart. Let them not disturb other Christians. In Jesus's name. Amen."

"Lake, do you think Jesus really would be driving a Jeep?" Zachariah seriously asked.

"Of course!" he answered and started laughing. Then he looked at Brisk, who began shaking her head, and she started laughing, and everyone joined in.

"A Jesus Jeep," Lawrence added." "His hair blowing in the wind. He'd be cool."

"Wonder what he'd look like," Zachariah asked.

"Seriously, I wonder how he had responded to those women," Lake thought out loud. "Keep them in your prayers. I think God has a message for us here. So far today we had Boss Hogg, then Mrs. Uppity Uppity, now the Loving Perfect Sisters. What is God trying to tell us? Everyone meditate on that today, and we'll share at the Eddy tonight."

"I think you were a little harsh with them, Lakeland," Brandy told him.

"Brandy, you think everything I do is harsh. You think I'm harsh with the grass when I'm mowing it. Chill out, they needed to be put in their place. Now, let's change the subject!

"Wow. Michael and Susan put up a lot of new artwork around the ice cream parlor. Look at those pictures of the wolves, Lake," Brisk said while pointing. "You like wolves."

"And there are some of arrows," Lawrence noticed. "They are tribal arrows. Michael is of Shawnee heritage."

"That's it, wolves, arrows! That's what it's been all day; wolves and arrows!" Lake fumed. "Matthew 7:15, 'They come to you in sheep's clothing but inside they are ferocious mangy old wolves!' And a verse I love, Psalm 91:5: 'You will not fear the terror of the night, nor the arrows that fly by day.' Wolves and arrows! We need to be aware of attacks from the enemy. We need to be on alert."

"What is a night terror?" Lawrence asked.

"You don't want to know," Lake responded.

"Are you serious, Lake?" Kenzie asks. "What should we do if you are serious?"

"We need to prepare our shields and bucklers," he replied.

"I know what the shield is, the shield of faith. But what is a buckler?" Zachariah asked.

"A buckler is a small shield. You can maneuver it around faster in the direction of an incoming arrow that you might suddenly see out of the corner of your eye. I think Psalm 91:4, 'His truth shall be your shield and buckler.'"

"Interesting," Lawrence said while in deep thought. "Look, I am sending you out like sheep among wolves, so be cunning as snakes and yet innocent as doves."

"That is awesome, Lawrence! That is truly awesome! Wow! Cunning as snakes yet innocent as doves. Something is going on. All right. See you all tonight at the Eddy," Lake told the group after his final spoonful of ice cream. "Don't forget to get a practice run in for the big race!"

Everyone said goodbye and headed to their various homes.

Lake got into his Jeep alone and said softly to himself, "Okay, Lord. What's going on?"

4

No One to Lead: A Father
to the Fatherless

A few weeks later, Lake was working on one of his mountain bikes when Kenzie stopped by at the cabin. "Hey, little bro!" he yelled to Kenzie.

"Hi, Lake. What are you working on?"

"Just adjusting the brakes. Guess what? I rented five bikes out today! Business is picking up. God is so good! What are you up to? Oh, you look serious."

Kenzie replied, "Well, I want to talk to you about something."

"Okay," Lake said while putting his tools down. "You have my full attention."

Kenzie sat on the steps while Lake sat on the porch, his back against the railing.

"Well, I know I have two more years of school. Um, you know I hate being so far away during the semesters, and I've been seeing Brandy for almost three years now. So—"

With a big smile on his face, Lake interrupted with "By all means!"

"Excuse me, I wasn't finished," Kenzie said, laughing. "You always know what I'm going to say. Now shut up and be serious for a change."

"Okay, I'm sorry. I'm honestly serious. Go ahead, Mackenzie," Lake replied, sensing the importance of the conversation.

Kenzie began nervously, "What do you think about, ah, at the Eddy tonight, if I, um." Then he paused for a few moments. "Okay, okay, Lake, you're my brother and my best friend. I, I bought a ring, and I want to propose to Brandy tonight at the Eddy. I want your blessing."

"Little bro, I'm so proud of you. Whatever you want, whatever it takes, I'm here for you, you know that. I'm 100 percent behind you. Of course, you have my blessing. Stand up!"

Both stood up facing each other. Lake placed his right hand on Kenzie's left shoulder and began praying, "Father, thank you for Mackenzie being my brother, he's the bestest brother ever. Please bless him and give him confidence with his decision. He asked for my blessing, but who am I? We ask for your blessings. Keep him strong and faithful. In Jesus's name. Amen."

"Thanks, Lake. You're the bestest brother. You know what? I've been thinking, maybe you should ask Brisk to marry you, and we could have a double wedding. I could be your best man and you could be my best man. Wouldn't that be cool?"

"Ask her to do what? And have a double what? I don't think those words are in my vocabulary. Brisk is my friend. She's not interested in me in that way."

"Wake up, Lake. All she talks about is you. She loves you. What are you waiting for?"

"She's probably like all the other girls. They end up thinking I'm too weird."

"Well, you are. But your real problem is, you won't let anyone get close to you. You just push them away then come crying to me when it's too late."

"Okay, that's enough Dr. Nidhatak. How's your car running?"

"Lake!"

"Kenzie! See, I can yell your name too. I can yell it louder. Listen… Kenzie! There, I win. Oh, I can see you're not amused. Okay, seriously, Kenzie today is your day. I truly want you to shine."

"Okay. I won't bug you but think about it. I care about you, Lake."

"Are you going to tell your father about your plans?" Lake asked.

"You mean your father? Yeah. I was going to stop by later tonight before coming to the Eddy. I told Brandy I was going to see your father, and I'd meet her before worship started."

"Tell your father his other lowly, no-good son said hello. Ask him to come visit. He's been here once in eight years. Of course, he said it was a dump and a pigsty. He always has a way with words. I can't believe you stay there when you're home from school. And people think I'm nuts."

"He's not that bad, Lake. He's a miserable old man, but I can handle it. Plus, it's only for a while longer. When Brandy and I set a wedding date, then I'll start looking for a place."

"Just be careful, I worry about you. But it sounds like you thought out all your options as usual. Good for you, little bro."

"I'll see you tonight, Lake. I love you, big brother."

"Drive carefully, see you tonight."

Later that night at the Eddy, guests were finishing their meal and prayer time was about to begin.

"McKenzie's not here, I'm a little worried," Brandy told Lake.

"He'll be here. He was stopping off at his father's house before coming over, remember?" Lake responded.

"That's being disrespectful, not saying he's your father."

"I didn't say that. All I said was Kenzie was stopping at his father's house. That's a true statement. No disrespect is intended. Listen, it's just brother-to-brother talk, kind of painful joking. I understand what you are trying to say, Brandy, I'm sorry. I just called Kenzie's cell but got no answer. Have the band continue the instrumental while we wait for Kenzie, and I'll clean up the tables." Brandy turned and walked toward the stage.

Just then, Lake's cell phone rang. Because of the people talking, he plugged one ear with his index finger and struggled to hear who was on the phone. "Kenzie? Kenzie! What's wrong? What! Lord, have mercy. I'll be right there."

Lake scanned the room. Seeing Lawrence talking to Pastor Bentley, he rushed over. "Listen, please, I got to go and pick up Kenzie. Please, Lawrence, do the prayer time and communion. I'll be back as soon as I can."

"I can't pray," Lawrence whined. "Ask someone else to do it?"

"This is an emergency! I don't have time to find anyone else right now! Just do it!"

"Pastor Bentley is right here, ask him."

"You know the rules, only us lower levels."

"Lake, what are you talking about?" Pastor Bentley asked.

"I just always want regular people to participate, mainly to develop their gifting. No offense, Pastor Bentley."

"No offense taken, Lake. I understand."

"Okay, okay, Zachariah, would you mind doing the prayer and communion since no one else has any, um, courage?" Lake said real fast. "You've been here before and observed. Would you mind?"

"I would enjoy that, Lake. Is everything all right?"

"No! Please don't say anything to Brandy, just pray. I'll be back. I gotta go!" Lake turned and walked quickly to the door to leave.

"Where are you going, Lakeland?" Brandy asked.

Without looking at her, he said, "I have to pick up Kenzie. I'll be back." Then he left.

*****

Lake pulled his Jeep into the driveway of his father's house on Otter Lake Road. He ran up the steps and walked inside without his usual polite knocking. There sat his father and his father's girlfriend watching a blaring TV. The room was full of cigarette smoke and empty beer cans covered the coffee table.

Lake's father looked at him and said, "Punk."

"Where's Kenzie?" Lake demanded. When he heard no response he screamed, "Where's Kenzie?"

"Here I am, Lake." Kenzie was leaning on the wall just outside his bedroom door. His face was bloodied, and one eye was swollen.

Lake rushed over. "Oh, little bro. God have mercy."

Kenzie slid down to the floor and began to weep. Before Lake could respond, his father walked up behind him and punched Lake in the side of his head, knocking him to the floor. Then he kicked Lake in the face. His father grabbed Kenzie and lifted him up. He went to punch Kenzie, but Lake stood in the way and got punched instead. Leaving Kenzie go, he punched Lake one more time.

Lake grabbed his father and shoved him against the wall. "Kenzie. Get what you can and get into my Jeep. Now!" Turning to his father, he told him, "That's the last time you'll ever hit Mackenzie. Do you understand?"

Lake's father burped into Lake's face, and then he said, "About time you sissies stood up for yourselves. All you two usually do is eat, sleep, and take up space. Just worthless punks."

"My Father in heaven happens to disagree with you," Lake responded. "To him, we're precious sons. We're children of the King. He loves us."

"Yeah, right." His father smirked. He struggled to punch Lake, but Lake was stronger and held him against the wall. "You are nothing but a loser, punk. You're a quitter. You're stupid. You'll wimp out in that stupid race you're planning on doing, just like last time. You can't do it, so why are you trying to drag everyone else into your worthless dream? You're a failure, a worthless failure. You'll never amount to anything. If you look at your life right now, you'll see what I'm saying is true. You are just a waste."

"I will finish the race. Why would you care anyway? You wouldn't bother to come see your sons run anyway? Would you?"

"I wouldn't waste the time," his father said.

"Listen," Lake pleaded. "Why do you hate us, we're your sons? Why did you do this? You used to be such an explorer, traveling around the world. When did you lose your vision? Was it Dawson? It wasn't your fault."

"Shut up, you lazy ass," his father yelled. "Neither one of you could compare to Dawson. Just go and never come back." Then he spit in Lake's face. "You think you're something, but you're nothing!"

Trying to control his anger, Lake looked intensely at his father and slowly said, "I'll do as you wish. When I leave, I'll never come back. But I want you to know that I know what you did to Mom. It took a few years, but I figured it out. The same thing you did to me when I was fifteen, except I lived!"

His father's grip relaxed, and he looked down toward the floor. Lake looked to his left, and Kenzie was standing there leaning on his backpack. The girlfriend was on the couch smoking a cigarette and watching TV as if nothing happened.

"Kenzie, go to the Jeep, I'll get your pack." Kenzie went outside and leaned against Lake's Jeep. Lake left his father's arms go and walked cautiously backward a few feet. He picked up Kenzie's backpack and walked to the door. He stopped at the door and with his back to his father he said, "All I want is to be a family. If you want to talk, please call me." A potted plant was flung in his direction and smashed against the wall by the door just missing Lake. Lake calmly walked outside slowly closing the door behind him.

Lake walked over to his Jeep. "Kenzie, where are you?" he yelled.

Kenzie came around the side of the house and replied, "I'm getting my stuff. After I called you, I decided I wasn't going to live under his roof anymore, so I packed up what little I had and threw it out my bedroom window. This is the last of it."

"Good thinking, Kenzie," Lake said as he placed Kenzie's backpack in the Jeep.

Lake hugged him, and Kenzie began to cry on his shoulder. "Why does he hate us, Lake, why does he hate us? I thought he'd be excited about me proposing to Brandy. He just went crazy."

"I don't know. I don't understand how anyone could hate their own sons. Stop crying. Big boys don't cry. Big boys don't cry. Do you understand? Look at me." Lake took his shirt off and began wiping the blood from Kenzie's face. "You got one deep gash on your left side of your face, one above your right eyebrow, and a big shiner. We're going to the hospital."

"No, I'm not. We're going to the Eddy, and I'm going to propose to Brandy as planned. I'm not letting any evil thing keep me from my goals. That's what you always tell me. Plus, I really want to go worship and pray with my friends."

"We can't go until you get cleaned up. They'll know you got hurt because your face is swelling. We'll skip the Eddy tonight."

"We're not skipping tonight, Lake, we're going."

"Kenzie, I don't want them to know."

"Know what?"

"I don't want them to know how he is," Lake said, pointing to the house. "I don't want anyone to know anything about our family life."

"Lake, do you think they won't notice my face tomorrow, or the next day or maybe the next? We can't hide it forever."

"Yes, we can. This is the last time it will ever happen, I promise you that."

"We're going to the Eddy and worship with our real family," Kenzie demanded.

Lake turned away. His anguish could be seen in his face. "Then you do the explaining," he said. "You know, you're getting as stubborn as me. But I know you love the Lord. We'll do as you wish... then to the hospital."

"We'll see about that."

"Come here," Lake said. He gave Kenzie a hug and held him tight. Just then, a big white luxury car drove by slowly.

"Who's that? What's he looking at? That looks like that Pastor Avalon," Kenzie said.

"I don't know, and I don't care. I'm only concerned about you, little bro. Let's get out of here."

A short distance down the road, Kenzie asked, "Lake, what did you mean when you said 'I know what you did to Mom.' What did he do to her and you?"

"Nothing. Now isn't the time."

"Lake, pull over now. We're going to talk."

Lake kept driving. "Kenzie, I didn't see you standing there. I said it in anger."

"But is what you said truth? Did something happen that I should know?" Kenzie asked but got no response. "Lake, this is not the way to the Eddy, turn around."

"I changed my mind. I told you I don't want anyone to know, we're going to the hospital."

"No, we're not!" Kenzie shouted. "Pull over. Pull over now!" Lake again offered no response then Kenzie grabbed the wheel and tried to steer the Jeep off the road. Lake hit the brakes and came to an abrupt stop.

Lake got out and slammed the door. "Go ahead and go to the Eddy! Call the newspaper, call the TV station, and tell the world our dirty laundry! He roughed you up a few times but never punched you like that before. I had years of it, and I don't want anyone to know!"

"Is that all you're concerned about?" Kenzie shouted back.

"Yes! No! I care about you. Yes, I don't want anyone to know, but you really need to go to the hospital, please."

Just then, a police car drove by and did a U-turn pulling in behind the Jeep with its emergency lights on.

"Now what?" Lake said agitated. "Thanks, Kenzie!"

A tall African American state trooper walked up alongside the Jeep. "Hi, Lake, I thought that was you when I saw the 'Jesus' bumper sticker."

"Ah, hi, Trooper Allen. Glad it's someone I know."

"Normally you call me John and now you say 'Trooper Allen'?"

"I'm showing respect for you and your position, that's all…sir."

"Kenzie! What happened to you?" John said as he rushed around the Jeep to Kenzie's side.

"Nothing, sir," Kenzie said.

"What's going on, Lake, you got blood too?"

"Please let it go."

"I'll decide when to let it go. Your brother has some nasty cuts. What happened? Were you boys fighting?"

"Not yet but pretty close," Kenzie told him.

"Our father" was all Lake could get out.

"Some father. Do you want to press charges this time?" John asked.

"This time?" Kenzie asked. "What do you mean this time?"

Lake shook his head no.

"This is too serious. He's gone too far. Now he's doing it to Kenzie too. He should have been locked up long ago. I'm sorry, but he was never much of a father to you boys. Do you want me to go talk to him, just talk?"

Lake reluctantly shook his head yes.

"You boys need to stay away for a while."

"We're not going back. We forgive, but we won't go back. David forgave Saul, but he stayed away from the palace," Lake said softly. "David wrote, 'When my father forsakes me, then the Lord will take care of me.' Kenzie and I know that God is the Father to the fatherless. He'll take care of us."

"You're right on all points, Lake. Where are you heading now, the hospital?" John asked.

"Uh, no, I guess we're going to the Eddy then to the hospital. Kenzie had some prior plans that must be taken care of first."

"Well, I'll swing by the Eddy after I talk with your father. I always wanted to stop in but I usually work weekend evenings. It'll give me a chance to check it out. I heard you do a fine job there, all of you."

"Not us, but the Holy Spirit. We just try to be obedient," Lake responded.

"I'll see you then, take it easy. boys."

"Thank you, sir," Lake said.

After John left, Lake looked at Kenzie and said with a grin, "I'm twenty-nine and you're twenty-two, and he still calls us boys." He went to start the Jeep and saw no keys. "What did I do with my keys?" He looked at Kenzie and Kenzie was holding them in his hands.

Kenzie said, "I thought I knew you pretty well, Lake, but I am thinking that there is probably more damage to your soul than to my face. We're not going anywhere until you tell me what happened when you were fifteen and what happened to Mom."

*****

42

Back at the Eddy, Zachariah finished prayer time and had celebrated communion. The band was finishing an hour of worship music. Kenzie drum set was noticeably empty. Lake quietly came in the side door so he wouldn't disrupt anyone worshiping. He found Pastor Bentley and stood beside him until the music ended. Then he tugged Pastor Bentley's sleeve and whispered something to him.

They both went outside the same way Lake came in.

Pastor Bentley walked over to Kenzie. Before he could say anything, Kenzie said, "Hi, Pastor Bentley. I know I look bad right now, but I'm fine, kind of. Listen, I want to propose to Brandy right now, but looking like this kind of messed up my plans. I don't know what to do. I don't want to distract from the service. Originally, I just wanted to say from the drums 'I have an announcement to make' and then do it. What do you suggest?"

"Can I ask what Lake suggested to you?"

Kenzie looked at Lake. "Well, he said he'd go in and explain to everyone our absence tonight and ask for prayer. Then I would come in make the announcement."

"Kenzie, Lake, you both need prayer tonight. That's what we are here for right? Let's do as Lake said, we'll have prayer and then, if you're up to it, make your proposal, Kenzie. I honor you for your strength and commitment."

All three went in the side door. Kenzie stayed in the back out of sight. At the right moment, Lake and Pastor Bentley went up front. Lake walked back to Brandy and told her Kenzie would be there shortly. Then, still wearing the bloodied shirt, he stood beside Pastor Bentley and faced the guests. "Hey, everyone. I'm sorry I wasn't here tonight. We had a family emergency, and um…" Lake was trying to hold his emotions. The building was quiet for several minutes. Pastor Bentley placed his hand on Lake's shoulder, but Lake stepped away. "You can do this Lake," Lake said to himself out loud. "Please, everyone, pray for Kenzie. My dad hurt him pretty bad tonight, and ah, he's here, but wants me to try to explain what happened before you see him because he's kind of messed up." Before Lake could finish, Kenzie walked up on the stage. Brandy rushed to him and hugged him. His face now was swollen and still bloody even though Lake tried to wipe away as much as he could. His shirt was torn and had bloodstains on it.

Pastor Bentley said, "Let all join in prayer for these young men. Please, everyone, come forward and let's lay hands on Lake and Kenzie. Everyone circled around them. Pastor Bentley opened the prayer, "Father, protect the children. Not only Lake and Kenzie, but anyone who may have been harmed by a family member. We pray for emotional healing and physical healing. We especially lift up these two brothers of ours."

Someone in the back prayed, "Thank you for Lake and Kenzie's desire to serve you, Father. Protect them."

An elderly woman near the front prayed, "Dear Jesus, protect these boys from any further harm. They are your children. Grant them strength to continue serving you."

A girl near the front softly spoke, "Heavenly Father, you are the God of the universe. Everything works together for good, according to your plans. Allow Lake and Kenzie to understand this trial and draw closer to you."

From the right side, a young man said, "You are God alone, there is none beside you. Thank you for our brothers, Lake and Kenzie. Keep them. Protect them. Bless them."

Then Lake and Kenzie looked behind them when they heard John Allen pray for them. As he placed his hands on their shoulders he prayed, "Father, comfort Lake and Kenzie. Their earthly father has caused them great pain, but as Lake said earlier, you are the Father of the fatherless. You love them more than any father could."

Pastor Bentley closed the prayer, "Father, we also pray for Lake and Kenzie's father. You know his heart. Soften his heart and draw him close to you and to his sons. Restore him and his family. In Jesus's name, amen."

Kenzie looked around and said, "Lake and I appreciate your love and prayers, everyone. Thank you for being here for us in our time of need, and I mean that with all my heart. I have something I want to say that was planned way before the events that took place tonight. I'm not going to allow what happened delay my plans. Good will triumph over evil tonight." He knelt down and faced Brandy. He looked into her tearful face and said, "Will you follow me through life seeking God to the utmost as Mrs. Mackenzie Nidhatak?"

"Mackenzie!" a startled Brandy yelled. Then she placed both of her hands on her face and stared at him. Everyone at the Eddy was cheering them on and praising God.

"Well?" Kenzie said as he held out an engagement ring in his hands.

"Yes! I want to follow you through life seeking God to the utmost as Mrs. Mackenzie Nidhatak!"

"Yes!" Lake yelled.

Kenzie painfully stood up and kissed Brandy then yelled, "Thank you, Jesus!"

Everyone clapped loudly as Brandy and Kenzie hugged. "Careful on the ribs, Brandy, I think a few are a little bruised."

The band began playing and the crowd joined in singing, dancing, and praising God. Throughout the night, friends and guests congratulated and prayed for Kenzie and Brandy. Lake sat behind the band, quietly watching the celebrating and contemplating the whole day.

After most everyone had left the Eddy, Brandy said to Kenzie, "We're going to the hospital, Mackenzie."

"No, I'm fine," he said. "I can deal with it."

"Mackenzie, we're going to the hospital, so get your stuff around," she replied.

"Oh, Kenzie," Lake said, laughing, "it sounds like you are married already!"

"Shut up, you crazy, hippy mountain boy," Kenzie said, also laughing.

"I'll get my Jeep ready and drive you to the hospital," Lake told him.

"We'll be fine on our own, Lake," Brandy said.

"But I really want to take you to the hospital, Kenzie, please," Lake pleaded.

"Lake, we'll be fine," Kenzie said while trying to get Lake to look at him. "Hey, don't look so disgusted. Brandy and I just got engaged and what a way to celebrate by going to the hospital together, right?"

"That's fine, really. I have a lot of work to do here anyway. Let me know when you get home, okay? We'll go get your Jeep in the morning. Here are my keys, oh, is that imposing also?"

"Lake," Kenzie said soft but stern.

"I sorry," Lake replied, "I just want to, I just wanted to, never mind, I'll see you later."

John interrupted them, "Kenzie, it's a good idea to go to the hospital. Those cuts need stitches. Lake, let Brandy take Kenzie, they'll be fine."

"You're right, I'm sorry," Lake replied. Turning toward Kenzie and Brandy, he told them, "Best you went to the hospital together and alone. After all, you two need to talk about tonight and your future. Wake me up when you get home, Kenzie. Good night."

"Good night, Lake," Kenzie said. "Thank you for being here, John. Thanks for praying. Good night."

"It was great to finally visit the Eddy. Good night," John replied.

Kenzie and Brandy began walking to the door.

"Lake," John began as he placed his arm around Lake, "your father wouldn't talk to me when I stopped. He slammed the door shut after he saw it was me. I don't want you going back there until I talk with him again. I don't want you or Kenzie ending up dead, do you understand?"

"Yes, sir," Lake said softly as he stared at the floor.

"The Lord is rooting for you. Lake, I believe you need to let the things of the past go. Everything. You had a rough night, and I want you to pray to forgive and to release everything to God. As you said earlier, 'David forgave Saul but he didn't go back to the palace.' So forgive and stay away."

"Yes, sir," Lake responded as John gave him pat on the back. "John, thank you for stopping by tonight. Thank you for everything. I wish you were—"

"What, Lake? You wish I were what?"

"I'm sorry, John. Never mind."

"I'm parked outback, so is it all right to go out the kitchen door?" John asked.

Lake nodded but didn't say anything.

Brisk, who was standing nearby watching, walked outside with Brandy and Kenzie. "Kenzie," she began, "I'll help Lake out tonight cleaning up, and I'll try talking to him."

"I don't think that's a good idea, Brisk," Kenzie said as he turned toward her on the porch.

"Why?" she asked.

"If you can get him to talk, go ahead," Kenzie answered. "But after all that has taken place tonight, oh, I think it may be a waste of you time. Maybe it's best you just leave him alone. That's my advice. We'll talk to you tomorrow, Brisk. Going to the hospital. Have a good night."

"Good night, Brisk," Brandy said.

"Good night and congratulations!" Brisk responded as she sat down on one the chairs on the porch.

A short time later, Lake walked outside and sat on the steps then began to pray out loud.

"Heavenly Father, thank you for making it through another day. Thank you for this beautiful night. Your stars are so beautiful. The aroma of your creation fills the air. The sound of your creation fills the air. You are wonderful to me. You've given me more than enough. You've blessed me more than enough. There is none beside you, none who can compare to your love and your greatness. Thank you for your mercies. I deserve death, but you give me life.

"Father, I pray for everyone who came to the Eddy that they found more of you tonight. Not by anything we've have done but because of what you have done. May we all live more for you, imitating Jesus.

"Father, I pray especially for my brother Mackenzie. Through him you brought me joy when I needed it most. I feel terrible what my dad did to him. If only I had forced him to move here long ago. Oh, forgive me God. Take all the pain from him both physical and psychological. But knowing him, he'll be fine. I pray no scars form on his face or in his heart.

"Bless him and Brandy. She's a little tough, but she does love you and Kenzie.

"I pray for the rest of the band, Brisk, Lawrence, little Parker, and Zachariah. Bless them all and expand their musical territory for the purpose of glorifying you.

"Oh, yeah, thank you for sending John Allen when I needed him. I don't know what would have happened between me and Kenzie if he hadn't shown up. He's a cool guy. Bless him God. I wish he was, never mind.

"Please show me what you want me to do. I'm so stupid I probably missed it. I'm not smart at all, God, so you may have to kick my butt to get my attention. Maybe drop a tree on my Jeep when I'm taking a leak.

"But I'm getting old, God, not much time left. I probably failed you already. You'll be yelling at me for eternity because I was so stupid and failed you miserably. I'm such a loser.

"If you can use me, please do. I just want what you want, but it seems like you just don't want me. No one does.

"I'm sorry, God. I just want you to hold me for a while. Please. In Jesus's name, amen."

He leaned back on the steps and stared at the sky for a few minutes. Then he sat up and sniffed the air. He said, "I can smell your perfume, Brisk. I thought you left."

"No, I said goodbye to Brandy and Kenzie then decided to sit down for a few moments. I was planning on coming in to help you clean up. I'm sorry if I startled you."

"You didn't startle me. I smelled your perfume and realized you were there."

Brisk walked over and sat beside him. "What's troubling you tonight, Lake?" she asked.

"Nothing," he responded. "I'm fine."

"Look at me, Lake," Brisk asked.

When Lake turned toward her, she began washing the bruises on his face with some tissues. "What happened earlier tonight?" she asked.

"I don't want to talk about it."

"Did this ever happen before? I've seen your face bruised several times since I met you, Lake. Why do you go back?" she asked.

He was silent.

"Lake, I'm not prying. I care about you. My heart hurts for you and Kenzie tonight. You don't have to tell me if you don't want to."

"It was just an isolated incident. My dad probably just had a bad day. Don't worry about it."

"Were all the bruises I've seen on you before caused by other isolated incidents?"

"I hit my dad's fist with my head. Not once, but several times. Are you proud of me?" He snarled at her.

"You were protecting Kenzie is what happened. You're a wonderful brother to him. I can see the close bonds you two have. You're afraid of losing that closeness, aren't you?"

"Yeah," Lake said as his eyes began to swell with tears.

"Lake, Kenzie is growing up. You'll always be part of his life. He'll always be part of your life. He said he'll name one of his sons after you."

"I think he meant he'll name a mangy old dog after me. Where is my mangy old dog anyway?" he asked while looking around.

"Sheba was sleeping on one of the bunks," Brisk responded. "I gave her some leftovers, but she wouldn't eat any of it. I asked her if she was okay, and she wagged her tail but did not lift her head. She must have had a rough day too."

"She hasn't been eating. She goes to the vet in a few days. It hurts to see her not being herself. Why does life have to be so hard?"

"One of my favorite phrases I got from you is, 'Life is hard, but God is so good, and the best is yet to come,'" Brisk said softly as she began again to gently clean his face.

"That's the problem," Lake told her. "Life had just started to be good since my mom and Kenzie came back to Mountain Springs four years ago. Prior to that, I hadn't seen him in over ten years. We were just separated brothers who then became the best brothers ever. We got even closer when my mom…ah…died. Now it is all going to change."

"You must believe it will change for the better, Lake," Brisk said. "Can you tell me about what happened when your folks split up?" Lake was silent. "Talk to me, Lake. What's on your heart?"

While Brisk gently cleaned Lake's bruised face, he began talking. "Well, we moved to Edmonton, Alberta, from Dawson City. I was about nine, and Kenzie two. After Dawson died my dad just gave up his dreams and tried to make it in the city. We were there a few years when I was told we were moving to Mountain Springs where my dad had relatives. We moved here, but my mom and Kenzie went south to her mom's relatives. My dad told me they were visiting, but they never came back. I later learned they had split up and, because they couldn't afford a divorce, divided everything up between them, including Kenzie and me."

"Why did your mom come back to Mountain Springs?" Brisk asked.

"My folks were trying to get back together, I guess. It was a fatal mistake on her part," he said.

"What do you mean by 'fatal mistake'?" she asked.

"Nothing! I'm sorry, I said too much," he told her as he stood up. "I'm sorry I don't usually talk about family. I don't like talking about family, I'm sorry."

"Lake, do you feel comfortable talking to me?" she asked.

"Yeah, I guess I do. It's kind of weird, I'm sorry," he said.

She hugged him and said, "Stop saying you're sorry. I'm glad you felt comfortable with me. It's getting late. I'll help you clean up, and maybe tomorrow night we can get together?"

"I don't know. Not sure if I want to face tomorrow," he replied.

"Lake, you don't believe those derogatory remarks your dad says, do you?"

"I try not to, but I think maybe he's right sometimes. I mean, look at my life? I'm nothing."

"I think you are something. So do a lot of people who came here tonight. The whole band appreciates what you've done for them."

"How's your car running?"

"You can't accept someone saying something nice about you, can you?"

"I'm just not used to it. I don't know when to believe it. Okay, enough interrogation."

"Lake, it's so beautiful here at night," Brisk said. "Listen to the crickets. You told us one time that they were praising God. I remember another time while we were standing on a stream bank watching the water drop over the rocks, and we could hardly hear, you said the waters were applauding God. I think you were right. You see God in ways most people don't."

"Why are you being nice to me?" Lake asked.

"You don't mind me being nice to you, do you?" she asked.

"I'm just not used to people being nice to me," he answered.

"Lake, I care about you. I like you. Is that okay?"

"Well, I guess. I don't understand why."

"Well, to be honest. Remember when we did the moonlight run and were back at the Eddy and you made fun of Kenzie kissing Brandy? I asked if you kissed like that and you jumped over the counter and kissed me, remember?"

"Yeah, I remember," he said with a slight smile.

"Well, that was the best kiss I ever had. That was a manly kiss I never thought possible. I saw you in a different light that morning. I've just been waiting."

"Waiting for what?"

"For you to ask me out."

"Why would you go out with me?"

"Why not?"

"Um, because you're beautiful, smart, can play music and sing like an angel. We have nothing in common."

"Okay, so you're asking me to go out Friday night. You said you'll pick me up about seven, is that right?"

"Well, okay, so that's a yes?"

"Well, let me think if I'm free that night. Yes, I am."

"Where am I taking you?"

"How about the Appalachian Café?" she replied.

"Okay, I guess that's a good choice on my part."

"Lake, I notice tonight John Allen seemed interested in what you do here at the Eddy and your life in general. Do you know him outside of church?"

"Oh, yeah. We have a long history."

"Were you in trouble with the law before?" she asked.

"Naw, nothing like that, just, ah, things like my dad and other stuff along the way."

"He's like a father figure to you, isn't he?"

"Yeah, he helped me out a lot of times. Yelled at me a lot of times. Gave me some counseling in church. I guess he is a kind of father figure to both me and Kenzie since we didn't have much of one. He is a great guy, very tough but fair. The best thing about him is he used to drive the church bus. He invited me to church, and he'd pick me up in his white church bus. One Easter, he sat me down and explained the gift of salvation. He's the one who led me to Jesus. If it wasn't for him, I don't know where I'd be. I wish he was my father."

"Did you ever tell him that?"

"No!"

"Tell me about the first time you met him," she asked.

"Oh, I don't know," he said.

"It must be a good experience, wasn't it?"

"I guess so. I remember I had a Little League game. It's the only game my dad ever came to. I don't know why he did. Anyway, I played third base and I remember him leaning against the fence yelling at me during the game like every move I made was wrong. I remember him even yelling I needed a haircut. Later in the game, John, who was an umpire, asked me some questions. I saw him go over to the fence and talk to my dad. He asked my dad if I could go to church, and the next Sunday, John came in this white bus, and I went to church for the first time."

"So what do you think John said to your father?"

"Ah, just baseball stuff, I guess. Yeah, John would be a cool dad," Lake said with a slight smile.

"Well, I can tell you who your father really is. Listen to this from the psalms," she said as she picked up her Bible and began to read, "Sing praise to the Lord! Raise you voice in song to him who rides upon the clouds! Jehovah is his name, oh, rejoice in his presence. He is the Father of the fatherless."

"Then in Mark 3:35 Jesus said, 'Anyone who does God's will is my brother, and my sister, and my mother.' He didn't say any of them were his father because there is only one father and that's the Lord God himself. He's your Father, Lake."

"I know that verse from Psalms. But sometimes I can't help but to wonder—"

"Wonder if God loves you?" she asked.

"Yeah," he answered.

"Lake, I can't believe you would think that. Of course he does."

"Then why'd he allow so much crap to happen? I mean, listen, I know he loves me. I just don't feel it. I just can't understand how he could like me. Even my own dad hates me."

"You dad doesn't hate you."

"Then what the hell do you call it?"

"I think it's time I go."

"I'm sorry, Brisk. It's been a long day."

"It's okay, Lake. I know you had a lot to deal with today and I know I was pressing you to talk to me. It's my fault. I just care about you." She gave him a kiss and a hug. "Call me tomorrow if you want to talk some more. Good night, Lake."

"Good night, Brisk," he said as he watched her walk to her car and drive away.

Looking at the starlit sky, Lake asked, "What are you up to, God? You know she's too good for me, that's for sure. I don't want to go through a relationship and breaking up again. Thanks for a beautiful night, God. Look at those stars! Got to go clean up the Eddy, good night." Lake turned and went into the Eddy and closed the door behind him.

5

Dreams vs. Nightmares

Kenzie and Brandy returned from the hospital about 2:00 a.m. Kenzie got out of the car and walked around to the driver's side. He kissed Brandy and said, "Drive carefully. I love you." He watched the car until the lights disappeared into the darkness. "Thank you, Jesus," he said out loud with a big smile then walked into the cabin.

Sheba began barking and prancing as Kenzie went inside. Kenzie orders her on the couch. She won't get up until he lifts her hind legs up. "You're one spoiled puppy," he told her, laughing.

Inside, he saw a note from Lake and read it, "Wake me up when you get home." Kenzie went into Lake's bedroom but didn't see him in the bed. Suddenly, he noticed Lake was lying on the floor. "Hey, what are you doing?" he asked. Lake didn't reply. Kenzie turned on the light. Lake was sweating profusely and was looking at Kenzie. Kenzie pulled Lake to a sitting position with his back against the dresser and then knelt beside him.

"Lake, can you hear me?" he asked.

"I'm okay now," Lake answered dazed.

"Was it a night terror?"

"I think, and the tower."

"The tower dream?"

"Yeah. Thank God it's over."

"Listen. I want you to tell me the dream, right now."

"I told you before."

"I know, but now it is fresh in your mind. Tell me," Kenzie said as he sat down beside Lake. "We know it's because of what happened last night. I'm sure that's what set it off. Tell me the dream…please."

Lake made a sigh then began. "The dream is a little different this time. It starts with me standing in front of…a house."

"Whose house?" Kenzie asked.

"You know!" Lake said upset.

"I'm sorry. Tell me the whole dream. Start with whose house."

"That pastor's. I remember it was a big new beige brick house, elbow-shaped, beautifully landscaped. I could see him walking around inside. I rang the doorbell and then hid in the shrubbery. When he came out, he looked around then walked down the sidewalk along the house to the garage. I stepped out between him and the front door. He saw me and said, "Hi, Lake, how are you?"

I had an M16 slung over my back, which I pulled over and pointed it at him. I said, "You should die." He was talking, but I could no longer hear him. I started shooting at him. The bullets were ricocheting all around him but not hitting him. He walked into the house smiling at me, completely unharmed. I was angry at myself for not killing him.

"Then what happened," Kenzie asked.

"I heard sirens. So I got on my motorcycle and took off. It was like I was going back in time. I went to our old house in Dawson. All the swings, the slide, the confidence course we built…all were gone…smashed, broken, destroyed. I looked in the house, and my piano was broken into thousands of pieces. I saw Mom's casket there. She was in it. She was dead, but I could hear her crying for help. Dad was sitting there…laughing. The presence felt so evil. That 'thing' was there. Kenzie, everything I remembered that brought joy was gone…destroyed."

"Lake, what thing?"

"The 'thing' that came into my room tonight! The night terror creature! Then I ran to the church for help. The moon was out then disappeared behind the clouds as I ran. The same thing, Kenzie. The same freaking thing! Everything that brought joy was…was like dirtied, defiled, destroyed. The piano, the youth room, everything!

Remember that big banner in the foyer that said 'Faith, Hope, and Love'? It was on the floor with dirty footprints on it. The footprints went into the pastor's office. I looked in and he was there…laughing…and the 'thing' was there too. I went outside and got on my motorcycle. I was going as fast as I could up some mountain road. It was foggy and misty, and I was crying. The road stopped at a tall communications tower. I started climbing up it. A short time later, I looked down and saw…"

"It's okay, Lake. Keep going."

Lake was trying to keep from crying but continued. "I saw the police, the district justice, the judge, the pastor, the church, and dad down there. Everyone was there. They were yelling terrible things at me. They all had guns.

"When I was halfway up, I looked to my left, and one of the red lights on the tower was right there in my face. My heart was pounding so hard, and the light was blinking at the same beat as my heart. There was something following me up the tower, but it wasn't human. It was that 'thing'! I couldn't exactly see it, but I could sense it. It was a black mist or something. So I tried to climb faster. I was climbing up on a metal ladder, but something kept knocking out some of the steps, making it needlessly harder to get to where I wanted to be.

"I was almost to the top. There was a larger red flashing light just above me. I was reaching out trying to get to the light, but that black thing was holding me back. I was reaching into the air for something, but I couldn't go any further. I was screaming out to the sky for help. But help never came. I wanted to climb to the top but couldn't. I thought if I could get there, I'd be safe. Finally, the thing let go of me. I climbed right up alongside the big red flashing light on the very top of the tower and held onto it with one arm and reached to the sky with the other. Whatever I had hoped for at the top suddenly disappeared. I felt this deep, deep hopelessness. I heard everyone laughing at me. I was holding on to the light with both arms, hugging it almost. It was as tall as me, and like the lower light, it was now blinking in sync to my pounding heartbeat. I could hear the pounding, but not sure if it was from me or the light.

"Then the thing put its head around the light and looked at me laughing. It touched me, and this horrid pain went through me. I wanted to throw up, it was a terrible feeling. The creature terrified me so much I slipped a little on the tower framework. The M16 trigger caught something, and a few rounds went off hitting me. Before I even reacted to the pain, everyone began shooting at me. I was hit all over and bleeding badly.

"I began to fall but caught a hold of one of the tower's crossbeams. I was dangling there only being able to hold on with one hand. With the other hand, I was trying to move the M16 so that I could shoot back. I didn't want to hurt anyone, just defend myself. I wanted them to stop hurting me and to stop laughing at me. But there was no way because the creature was kicking the M16 and laughing. I yelled, 'I'm innocent.'

"Then I began to fall again. It seemed like a long time. About halfway down the tower, I got tangled up in electrical wires. I couldn't breathe or move. I felt so vulnerable to the creature. I felt it was coming down the tower to destroy me. It seemed like I was struggling so hard inside me, but outside, I couldn't move. I couldn't yell or make a noise, but inside I was screaming for help. Something was holding me, and I was suffocating. I was in so much pain and couldn't breathe. I felt such an evil presence. All of a sudden, I began falling. Everyone was smiling with joy. Then I woke up before I hit the ground.

"After yesterday, I knew I should have closed and locked my bedroom door so 'it' couldn't get in. But I wanted to hear you when you got home."

"Well, Lake," Kenzie began, "we know why you have this dream. We believe God's word from Psalms that you will not have to worry about the 'terrors in the night' anymore. We claim it tonight in Jesus's name. Right?"

"Right," Lake softly replied. "No more night terrors."

"What's this you wrote on your dream pad?" Kenzie asked.

"What's it say?"

"Army, Sheba, John. Were these tonight?"

"I don't know right now. I can never tell. I don't remember. I can never sleep straight through, and you told me to write down the dreams. I guess I was up a lot tonight waiting for you to get back."

"Tell me the army dream again," Kenzie asked.

"Same army dream. I'm dressed in some kind of uniform that I didn't want to be in. I think it's army. I hated it. I'm always the lowest-ranking one there. I'm packing up all my equipment as if going off to war, and I know I'm going to die. Everyone is so nasty to me. They hate me. They won't let me eat or sleep. I have to pack an airplane for the others by myself, but I'm not going on this plane. They are getting out of the army and going on vacation. I'm going off to war.

"Sometimes I'm in this big building with lots of brass. That's generals and colonels and big guys. No one hears anything I say. I'm yelling at them just trying to get their attention because I have something important to say, but they are so busy talking amongst themselves and telling each other how wonderful they are that they don't hear me.

"Then I was in the back of a deuce and a half. That's a two-and-a-half-ton truck. I was there all by myself going off to war. I knew I was going to die. But no one cared.

"Then the worst part. I realized my enlistment had ended, and I reenlisted! I didn't remember I reenlisted. I was just there. I was screaming at myself, 'Why? Why? You hated this, and you reenlisted. You could have been free! Now four more years!' I told myself it was a dream and begged to wake up, but I couldn't. It was sickening real. I couldn't wake up, and it seemed like forever. After I finally did wake up, it was such a relief. I was like, 'Thank God, it was a dream.'"

"Are you happy here at the cabin and doing the Eddy?" Kenzie asked.

"You know I love it," Lake replied.

"Are you happy at church?"

"You know the answer to that."

"Do you feel some people in authority should not be in that position?"

"You know the answer to that."

"When things go wrong, like yesterday, are you blaming your-self and figuring there is no way out, and it may be years until there is any solution?"

"I don't know."

"Tell me about the Sheba dream."

"Well, that is new. It started out sad then it got kind of beautiful then real sad. I think it was because she is sick, and I'm taking her to the vet soon. I think I'm worried.

"It started out I was in the city with her. Then I lost her. I looked all over the place for her. Ran in and out of stores looking. The traffic was really bad, and I was worried sick she might get hit by a car. After a while, I saw her running on a street going up a hill. I ran after her and caught up to her. She looked at me and smiled. I smiled back and reached over to pet her. I was running evenly with her, and we were loving it but there was something sad at the same time.

"We kept going up and up on a long and winding road. There was less and less traffic. Less and less houses. I noticed all the build-ings were white now, earlier they were grey. We kept running and laughing. It was so almost perfect. It was like the good old days when her, and I would sneak off Sundays and go for a long run, just her and me. We always had so much fun. She was so fast and powerful.

"Anyway, in the dream we ran and ran, higher and higher. At one point we were high above the city, only open fields full of wildflowers. Then we came to a church. No one was there. We ran around the church a few times, like hide-and-seek. She played it well. I was laughing and laughing. I was so happy. She made me enjoy life so much.

"Then suddenly she stopped ahead of me. She looked at me seriously. Just stared. A tear in her eye rolled down her face. I knelt down, and she came and licked my face. I wanted to touch her, but I couldn't move. She barked once and looked up toward the field behind her as she wagged her tail slowly. She looked intensely at me again and whined a little. She barked again. Then she turned around and ran up the field about fifty feet. She turned and looked at me again. I couldn't move. I wanted to follow her so bad. But I couldn't move!

"The field was full of flowering blue chicory. She looked so beautiful standing there, the flowers all around her. I wanted to hold her so bad. She barked twice at me. Then she turned and ran up the field. Kenzie, I knew I was never going to see her again. Way, way out she stopped and looked back. Then she turned and ran out of sight. I cried and cried.

"I turned and started to go into the church and, maybe, talk to someone. But as soon as I opened the door, a cold stale breeze came out. It was so cold. I knew no one in there would understand. I didn't want to bother anyone. I thought they'd laugh at me. Oh, Kenzie, it hurt so bad. I just wanted someone to trust and talk to."

"Kenzie, do you think she's going die on me?" Lake asked as the tears streamed down his face. "I couldn't bear life without her."

"I don't know, big bro," Kenzie answered with sadness in his tone.

"She hasn't eaten for days now and I'm worried," Lake told him.

"I know, Lake. I know. I can tell by the dream you are worried. Wait and see what the vet says."

"Before you and Mom came back to Mountain Springs, she was the only thing flesh that I knew loved me and the only thing flesh that I knew I loved."

"I know, Lake. Um, tell me about the John dream."

"I just remember going up the steps into church. The music was heavenly. Pure spiritual worship. The church was packed. I had a wife and a bunch of kids and was so happy. You walked in beside me with Brandy and a bunch of kids too. You had decided to stay in Mountain Springs. The whole band was married, and everyone had kids. You and the band were up there playing, and some of your kids were playing too. Some of mine were. It was so beautiful. We all were so happy.

"Then I saw John up there where the pastor usually sits. He wasn't all dressed up, just the usual John. Then he got up to preach, and wow, it was solid Bible teaching. He was the pastor! Whatever the Lord placed on his heart is what he preached. No year-long series or the ten-point plan with five subcategories under each one. He was preaching the Word of God.

"Then they had an altar call and lots of people were going down to surrender their lives. It was so wonderful. People were dancing and praising God. No one wanted to leave."

"That's a confusing one, Lake. I mean, it's a happy dream, but why would John become the Pastor?"

"I don't know, Kenzie. But he sure would be a good one."

"About me and Brandy staying, that's just hopeful thinking on your part. Right?" Kenzie asked with a smile.

"I guess," Lake replied.

"Then you had the tower dream, right?"

"Yeah. Before the tower dream, I woke up and was thinking about last night, and I could sense 'it' was in the house. I hoped you get back early. Then I fell asleep and had that dream. Now here we are. Hey, your stitches don't look too bad. I was worried. Looks like ten stitches?"

"No, close. I got twelve."

"Does it hurt?"

"Not too bad. Got a good headache. They gave me some pills to sleep tonight."

"Can I have some? I want to sleep good for a change, please."

"Lake, what do you think set Dad off last night?"

"Well, Kenzie, I thought about it. I don't know for sure, but I think because you told him you were proposing to Brandy and was going to be happy in life. He's never happy. Plus, the booze turns the nasty old man into a nastier old man. I don't know. I don't want to talk about anymore."

"Do you think he's mad about something?"

"Kenzie, I don't want to talk about anymore right now."

"But...why not?"

"Because it will bring me nightmares. Because it will bring me night terrors. Because it will bring me pain. They hurt so bad, these stupid dreams. I just want them to stop. It's the only time I feel weak. Listen, there is nothing we can do so let's not talk about it anymore."

"Here's two of the pills. I'm only giving you them once and just so you can sleep, all right? Don't ask me again." He handed Lake two of the pills, and Lake swallowed them immediately.

"Kenzie, sometimes at night, I'm so tired I just want to drift off to a nice long sleep and forget some things. Sometimes I know 'it' is in the house, and I'm afraid to go sleep."

"You know, 'it' is a figment of your imagination," Kenzie explained. "A night terror is psychological. Don't give credit to something that does not physically exist."

"I know, Kenzie. But that's the best way I can describe it."

"Well, Lake, get up and get into bed. It's late, and I'm tired. You sound better then when I first talked to your tonight."

"Yeah, I'm tired too. Hopefully, I can get a good night's sleep now. Pray for me Kenzie, please. Pray for a good night's sleep."

"Okay," Kenzie said with a mischievous smile. "Now I lay me down to sleep—"

Lake interrupted the prayer. "Listen, Dr. Bastard, cancel the prayer. I'll do it myself," as he started to laugh. "Hey, what's that on your face? Stitches?"

"Ouch! You hippie bastard! That hurt!" Kenzie yelled as he stood up. He saw a glass of water on the nightstand, dumped it on Lake's head, and then ran out of the room.

Lake stood up as Kenzie looked back in. "Hey, Kenzie. Thanks for making me laugh when I needed it. Come here."

"I don't trust you, Lake. You're going to get me back, aren't you?" Kenzie said, laughing.

"No, little bro. You won with the water tonight. Just watch your back! Let's go out to the kitchen, I need a drink." As they walked out, Lake continued, "Seriously, thanks for being here. You're the only family I have now."

"Hey, same here, Lake. Kind of sad isn't it. But our future is in God's hands. I know this crazy hippie who always says, 'Life is hard, God is good, and the best is yet to come.' Do you believe that?"

"Yup. Just one question for you," Lake replied as he got out two glasses, and Kenzie poured orange juice into each one.

"What that's, Lake?"

"What's a hippie?"

"I'm not sure," Kenzie answered going into a deep serious thought. "I think it's a yuppie's grandfather. Yeah. I think it's hippies, yippies, and then yuppies, then maybe guppies."

"No! Guppies are fish. What do they teach you in college?" Lake asked, laughing.

"Yappies? Yappies?"

"No, they're televangelists. And you got a four-year scholarship?"

"Shut up!"

"Hey! Toast?" Lake asked while holding up his glass.

"I don't want toast."

"No! Man, you must be tired and dazed! Usually, I'm the dense one. Are you okay?"

"Shut up!" Kenzie said, laughing. "I'm punched, stitched, drugged, and in love."

"Yeah, you're one pitiful mess. That reminds me, when you plan the wedding, tell Brandy I only wear blue. Only. Now, let's toast to your future...our future."

"Oh, that kind of a toast. I'm hungry now...for toast."

"As I as saying, here's to living for Yahshua!

"Yahshua! Peace, Lakeland!"

"Peace, Mackenzie."

"Peace, Dawson," Kenzie added.

"Peace, Mom," Lake replied.

Both looked at each other and in sync said, "Peace, Dad."

"Good night, Kenzie."

"Good night, Lake."

6

Rain, Reign

Lake was cooking breakfast when Kenzie staggered out of his bedroom. "What time is it?" he asked.

"It's 7:21 a.m. Why are you up, Kenzie?"

"I smelled the coffee and then the bacon. I couldn't resist. How'd you sleep?"

"Real good. How about you?"

"Okay, I was in and out of it. I still have a headache."

"Well, here you go! This will make you feel better. Eggs, bacon, and some peaches. Thank you, Lord, for our breakfast and for your peace."

"Thank you, Lord. Thank you, Lake."

"Hey, Kenzie, it's been a week since you moved here. Do you miss dad's place?"

"Um, no. Not at all. I like the quiet here. No smoke, no TV, no yelling. I should have listened to you long ago. Plus, the coffee is good!"

"Thanks. I enjoy you being here. Actually, it's been fun. Hey, I was wondering, where are you going for your honeymoon? Have you decided yet? You always have a plan."

"Actually, I do. I didn't tell Brandy, yet I want to go to Yellowknife in the Northwest Territories. Remember you and I talked about driving up there a few years ago? I thought about it recently, and I decided that would be a great adventure. Yellowknife is out in the wilderness but has the comforts of a small city."

"Yellowknife! I always wanted to go there. Can I—"

"No!" Kenzie abruptly answered then laughed.

"I'm joking!" Lake said, laughing.

"Well, I hope so!" Kenzie replied. "Hey, what are your plans for today?"

"Splitting firewood this morning before it rains."

"Need help?"

"Oh, little one, it's a man's work. I'm not sure you can handle it."

"Hahaha. I bet I can split more in an hour than you could!"

"Oh, you know better than to give me a challenge! You're on! Loser buys the winner dinner!"

"What time this afternoon do you want to start?"

I said, "This morning, before it rains, 8:00 a.m."

"Eight?"

"Are you changing your mind, Kenzie?"

"No, but… I…okay! Eight. You are on!"

"Eight it is. I am going to get a shower and get ready. See you at eight, Kenzie. Dress properly and bring a sharp axe!"

"I'll be ready, old man!"

"Fine!"

"Double fine! Hey, breakfast is good. Thanks, Lake."

At 8:00 a.m., Lake was standing at the pile of unsplit wood waiting for Kenzie. He was wearing overalls with no shirt. He placed gloves on and checked the sharpness of the ax-head. The axe had a blue fiberglass handle.

Kenzie came out of the cabin wearing shorts and no shirt.

"Where's your axe, little lumber boy?" Lake asked.

"Oh, silly one, why would a psychologist have an axe? Maybe one of his patients but not me. And I know you know that so where is one of your spare axes?"

"Here, this is fiberglass and a little lighter for those fragile arms of yours."

"Shut up! Let's go!"

"Kenzie, seriously, you should get some pants on and a shirt."

"Why?"

"Did you ever split wood before?"

"I think I did, I think."

"Well, sometimes the pieces fly, and it could hit your legs or your chest. So maybe get some more clothing protection. I don't want you to get hurt anymore."

"I'm fine! You're just trying to distract me. Now, what's the plan, Lake?"

"Well, we'll split the wood and then pile it on the front porch of the Eddy, against the wall. Don't block any windows. You pile to the left of the front door, and I'll pile to the right. Both sides are the same. Any questions?"

"Do I split it all first and then pile it?"

"Whatever you are comfortable with, Kenzie. I split a bunch and then pile it. That way I don't get too bored, and my body is moving differently almost all the time."

"Okay. I'm ready, Lake. Let's go."

"Let's go! Be careful. We'll stop at ten."

Kenzie and Lake began splitting wood. After five minutes, both were sweating profusely in the humid morning air. Lake stopped splitting and began to carry his wood to the Eddy's porch. Kenzie, keeping a learning eye on Lake, did the same. He noticed what Lake had neatly arranged on the porch was much more than his shaky pile. So he began to work faster.

"Ouch!" Kenzie yelled after a piece of wood hit him in the knee.

Lake looked at him and smiled, trying not to utter "I told you so."

Kenzie yelled, "Shut up!"

"I didn't say anything!"

"Yeah, but you were going to!"

"Do you want a Band-Aid and an ice cream cone?"

"Shut up!" Kenzie yelled while laughing. "I'm going to beat you at this!"

"Take a break, Kenzie. Here's some water."

"Thanks, Lake. This is a workout."

"That's why I love it. You ready?"

Kenzie took a gulp of water. "Okay already! Let's go," he said enthusiastically.

At 9:50 a.m., Lake was far ahead of Kenzie who looked exhausted. Both men were soaked with sweat and covered with dirt, sawdust, and pieces of bark.

"Should I wait for you to catch up?" Lake asked.

"This is hard. You won, Lake."

"No, we have ten minutes, let's go."

Kenzie hesitated but then began splitting more wood. Lake carried wood to Kenzie's side of the porch. At ten o'clock, both sides were even.

"Why'd you do that, Lake?"

"Because you are my brother. Because we are a team. Neither one is better than the other."

"You're the bestest brother, Lake. Thanks."

"No, you are the bestest brother. I really enjoyed that."

"Let's go another hour, Lake. I can do it."

"I have no doubt, but I got to take Sheba to the vet."

"Okay, you won. I'll buy you dinner."

"Cool. And I'll buy you dinner."

"But you won, Lake!"

"Nobody won. I'm just more used to doing this. We each did what we were capable of. We each gave it 100 percent. Keep trying for a few weeks and build up those, um, muscles. Then we'll compete."

"Shut up!"

"Hey, an Eddy Lumberfest! That would be fun. Kenzie, help me pull this tarp over the pieces we didn't split. Supposed to rain hard this afternoon. Tropical storm Elvira is heading straight toward Mountain Springs. I got to get washed up and Sheba ready. We'll finish this pile tomorrow."

A few hours later, Kenzie was reading at the table while a heavy rain could be heard pounding on the roof of the cabin. He barely heard the knock on the door. Walking to the window to look out, he then quickly turned and rushed to the door. "Come on in, Brandy, I wasn't sure if I heard a knock or not because of the rain. Sorry!"

"Good afternoon, Mackenzie," she said as she kissed him. "Thanks for calling me for lunch. I got the message as soon as I got home from work. I am tired."

"Where's Lakeland? Isn't he back from the veterinarian yet?"

"No. It's been four hours since he left. She didn't move much this morning. Hardly lifted her head when he called her."

"How's Lakeland doing?"

"Well, we chopped wood this morning and had a great time. He was his old self, and as usual, he beat me at splitting but made me feel his equal. He's such a good brother and friend. We had fun. Look at the piles of wood on the porch of the Eddy we split!" Kenzie said as he pointed out the window toward the Eddy.

"You guys did a lot of work, Mackenzie. But you should be taking it easy with those stitches for a few more days."

"Then when Lake came in and got ready to take Sheba to the vet, he didn't say much. That's when I know he's hurting. She's been around for twelve years, eight years before I moved here. She was his best friend and a companion on all of his trips. He'd say, 'She's the only thing I knew I loved and the only thing I knew loved me.' It's going to be hard."

"I know, Mackenzie. When I first saw Lakeland driving around in his Jeep and Sheba there with her seatbelt on, well, I knew she had to be special to him."

"She went downhill so much in the last few days, though," Kenzie told her. "Tuesday, she stumbled down the steps. That broke his heart. It made him so sad to see her get so weak. Last night, he carried her out and had to hold her steady while she peed. That's the last time she got up. Hey, I think I heard him beep his horn."

As Kenzie open the front door, he grabbed an umbrella and rushed out to Lake's Jeep.

"Well?" he asked as Lake got out. Lake pointed to the other side of the Jeep as he walked around.

"Hold that above her please. Keep her dry." Lake reached in and picked up a sleeping Sheba, wrapped in a quilt. Kenzie stayed tight against Lake, trying to keep Lake and Sheba dry. Brandy held the door open as they came up the steps and onto the porch. Kenzie dropped the umbrella and followed Lake into the house. Lake stopped, looked around, trying to decide where to place Sheba. Then he walked into his bedroom and laid her on his bed.

"Kenzie, will you get me the phone and the number to the church's prayer line?" Lake asked. While Lake waited, he knelt down so he could be face-to-face with Sheba. As he petted her, all that he could hear was the heavy rain. He felt the warmth from her shallow breaths on his face.

"Here you go," Kenzie said as he handed the phone to Lake. "It's dialing for you."

"Hi. Is this the South Brook prayer line?" Lake asked softly. "Um, this is Lakeland Nidhatak. I was wondering, um, if you could pray for my dog Sheba. She is dying. She has liver cancer. What?" Lake placed his hand over the receiver. "Kenzie, it's Justin. He said they don't pray for dogs." He took his hand off the receiver. "Justin, um, she's important to me." Lake slowly laid the phone down on the bed. Without removing his face from Sheba's, he said, "Kenzie, he's laughing at me. Justin's laughing at me. He said 'Get over your stupid dog.'"

Kenzie said, "Why on Earth would Justin Bentley be handling the prayer line!" He grabbed the phone and walked out of the bedroom. Brandy was standing at the bedroom door. "Excuse me a minute, Brandy," he said to her as he passed by. "I need to correct someone."

Kenzie walked out onto the porch and closed the door. Brandy and Lake could hear his loud voice but were unable to distinguish what he was saying as he paced back and forth. After ten minutes, he came back into the cabin and laid the phone down on the table.

"Lake," he began softly as he walked into the bedroom, "Pastor Bentley will be over sometime this afternoon to see you and pray for you and Sheba."

"I don't need prayer," Lake responded. "Only Sheba does. I don't want to see any of the Bentleys. Besides, I won't be here. She's sedated and will be out for most of the day. I need this time to think about something, so I want to go somewhere by myself."

Kenzie, knowing what Lake had to think about, walked over, and knelt beside Lake then placed his arm around him.

"What is it, Lake? What do you have to think about?"

Lake grew tense and his breathing increased. "They suggested I put her to sleep."

"Oh, Lake," Kenzie said, pulling him close. "Oh, man. Lake, big brother. Um, they know best. Lake, they don't want her to suffer. They don't want you to suffer."

"But what if she gets better?" Lake asked.

Kenzie was at a loss for words for a few minutes.

"Lake, look at her," Kenzie said, teary-eyed. "I'm so sorry but look at her. Her gums are yellow, her eyes are yellow. You said she has cancer on her liver. Her liver has failed. Lake, her liver has failed."

Lake didn't respond.

Kenzie looked at Brandy and mouthed "pray" and pointed to Lake.

Brandy walked over and sat behind the brothers. She placed a hand on Kenzie shoulder, a hand on Lake's shoulder and began to pray. "Father, I pray for Lakeland's heart. Ease his pain. Ease Sheba's pain. We know the hard decision he needs to make shortly. I pray you gently guide him. Grant him strength. In Jesus's name. Amen." She pulled everyone together into a big hug.

"Thanks, Brandy," Kenzie told her as she returned to the doorway.

"Lake," Kenzie began, "you always say, 'Life is hard, but God is good, and the best is yet to come'—"

Lake interrupted him. "The best already came and now two of the three nearly gone. Soon the third. Then what?"

"What are you talking about, Lake?" Kenzie asked. "I don't understand."

"I don't understand either. I don't understand life. I don't understand God! Listen, when you and Mom come back to Mountain Springs, I mean, the last few years have been the happiest of my life. Then mom died, now Sheba's leaving, and soon you're getting married and leaving too. Then what? Then what!"

"Lakeland Nidhatak, Jesus said he'll never leave you nor forsake you. As I strive to be like him, I will never leave you nor forsake you. Do you understand?"

"I'm going for a long run. I have to," Lake told Kenzie.

"Lake, it's supposed to rain hard all day, a tropical storm system is pushing through."

"All the better, Kenzie. Eighty degrees and rain, all the better. Watch Sheba for me, please," Lake said as petted Sheba and kissed her. "I'm going to the Meadows." He went out the front door and left in his Jeep.

Lake began driving to a place called the Meadows. A wilderness area full of wetlands, waterfalls, and miles of seldom used trails. He came to a secluded parking area and turned off the jeep. After staring out the window into the woods for several minutes, he got out. He tied his key in the lace of one of his running shoes, removed his shirt, and placed a ball cap on. He began hiking down a trail alongside a creek. The rain was torrential, and shortly, his hat, running shorts, and running shoes were soaked.

The trail paralleled the creek for several descending miles down a spruce filled valley. Small cascades raced downstream as Lake began to run alongside. Seeing a big puddle on the trail, Lake jumped and splashed himself, resulting in a childish laugh.

Lake came to a twelve-foot waterfall. After walking into the pool below the falls, Lake carefully backed into the thundering water, which heavily massaged his shoulders. Holding his hat, he dove underwater away from the falls. Turning on his back and pushing himself to shore, he stared at the water pounding loudly into the pool directly in front of him.

Climbing out of the pool, he began running the best he could down the creek, splashing and sometimes falling. The water came to a big reservoir behind an old dam. Lake ran around the northern side and came to the dam. As he illegally crossed the breast of the dam he began running as fast as he could because he knew he had three separate ten-foot outlets to jump.

After the third successful jump, he stopped to look back at his achievement. The raindrops were shattering the surface of the water.

Lake looked toward the foggy mountains and the dark, rain-filled sky. "So beautiful," he said in praise. He then jumped into the water and swam to shore.

Finding an old railroad bed, Lake began running downhill along the creek again. Coming around a slight bend, he stopped at the sight of a lynx in front of him. The lynx turned and for several second examined Lake as Lake examined the lynx. Quickly it disappeared into the woods. Lake continued and crossed the creek over a shaky abandoned railroad trestle. A short distance later, he began walking as he ascended to Rainbow Ledges.

The trail up to Rainbow Ledges was now a torrent of muddy water. Lake walked directly through the water, enjoying the coolness and the resistance. At the ledges, very little could be seen, the rain and the low clouds shrouded the views. But it didn't matter because it was still beautiful to Lake. After looking at the pools of water filling the depressions on the ledges, he began running the trail through the woods. Several deer were disturbed, and white tails could be seen for a moment as each disappeared in various directions.

Lake stopped and turned around after hearing something strange. As he looked into the woods, he saw two porcupines were facing each other upright as if dancing. They would touch hands and then drop to the ground and repeat it all the while they were chanting a strange sound Lake never heard before. He watched this amazing performance for several minutes then concluded it was some mating dance and decided to let the lovers alone.

The rain slowed, and occasional thunder echoed through the mountains as Lake ran along a narrow muddy fire road. Coming over a small hill, he saw his goal for the day: a knoll and its unnamed lake. He slowed as he ran alongside the blueberry-covered shoreline. At the access road across the earthen dam, he walked to the furthest side. The open mowed field overlooked the lake and surrounding wilderness. Lake knelt and prayed silently. Thunder again could be heard at a distance.

Lake walked to the shoreline and into the water. Up to his neck in the warm water, he stood still and listened to the rain pattering the surface of the water. The rain became heavier and became a downpour. The collision of the falling rain and the lake's surface was one of Lake's favorite sounds.

"Don't just rain on me, Lord, reign in me!" he pleaded. "Reign in me! Please." He noticed the pressure of the water pressing against his body. "Is that you holding me? Hold me, Jesus, just hold me a little while." The heavy rain continued, and Lake stayed stationary, unwilling to leave the beauty of God's creativity at such a rare moment. Thunder shook the air.

"Lord, you reign, let the earth be glad. Let the distance shores rejoice! Clouds and thick darkness surround you. Righteousness and justice are the foundation of your throne. Fire goes before you and consumes your foes on every side. Your lightning lights up the world. The Earth sees and trembles. The mountains melt like wax before you. The heavens are declaring your righteousness! Rain on me and reign in me! I rejoice in you, Lord…and I give thanks. Thank you for this moment. Thank you."

The rain slacked and Lake reluctantly swam to the shore. He walked across the dam and back to the road. He turned around and pondered the dam. He knew this was the perfect resting place for Sheba. His thoughts were now focused on what he was avoiding all day…reality. Sadness enveloped him as he turned and walked down the hill into the woods. He walked the five miles back to his Jeep in the rain.

Nearing the parking lot, it was getting dark. The clouds opened slightly, and Lake saw the moon in its waxing gibbous phase. Lake gave a dim smile as the clouds quickly covered the moon again and a light rain began. "Thank you for allowing me to see the moon. I know you're with me, Father. Thanks."

Lake came to his Jeep and got in. After a few minutes, he got out and leaned his back against a tree. He closed his eyes as he heard the rain in the trees. Slowly he sunk to a sitting position against the tree, his lower body into a puddle. Tears flowed as heavy as the earlier rain. "I don't want this day to end. I don't want to go home. Oh, God, help me," he cried from the heart. He lay down in the puddle and cried uncontrollably.

He heard a noise and looked up. "Kenzie?"

Kenzie pulled him up. "Let's go home, Lake." Lake nodded, affirming Kenzie's desire. Brandy dropped me off, and I hung around your Jeep. "Are you okay? Were you crying?"

"I'm saturated, and you ask if I've been crying? Big boys don't cry."

They got into the Jeep, and Kenzie drove. Heavy rain and the splashing of the Jeep through puddles was all that could be heard. Then Lake said, "I saw a lynx, a coyote, deer, porcupines facing each other, making noise. It was beautiful. I swam at the dam and the knoll. The rain was hitting the water so hard. It was so beautiful. I didn't want to come back. I didn't want to come back, Kenzie. I almost forgot everything. I didn't want the day to end."

Kenzie listen without saying a word as Lake guardedly spilled his heart. On the way home, the rain stopped. Lake wondered out loud, "Maybe I should set up my tent and sleep out with Sheba tonight. Kind of like when we were backpacking. One final camping trip."

"We think alike, Lake. The tents already up behind the cabin," Kenzie told him.

"Thanks, Kenzie."

After eating and getting dried, Lake took Sheba to the tent and gently laid her beside him. Kenzie knew he wanted to be alone with Sheba, so he prayed with Lake and went to bed. Lake wrapped his arm around Sheba and watched the sky. As it cleared, he gazed at millions of stars and the moon. He held Sheba and listened to her breathing as he dozed in and out of sleep.

Early in the morning, he woke as Sheba took her last breath. "Oh, baby. I'm so sorry," he yelled, realizing he allowed her to suffer. "I didn't know you were that bad. I'm so sorry. I'm so sorry."

Lake gently ran his hand across her face and back as the moon made her white fur look so pure. He took her into the cabin and covered her up on the couch as if she was just sleeping.

Kenzie came out of his room. "She's gone," Lake told him. "Walk down to the Sheba Falls with me?"

Kenzie got dressed and met Lake on the front porch. They walked down to the falls, neither saying a word. As they sat on rocks facing the moon, Lake prayed, "Father, thank you for Sheba not suffering anymore. Thank you for it being over. I'm sure you'll love her running around heaven with you. She's so precious."

"Thank you for the twelve years. You allowed me to spend with her. She brought me so much joy. I can't thank you enough. She the bestest. Absolutely the bestest. Thank you."

"Are you all right, Lake?" Kenzie asked.

"Yes. It's over. No more suffering. I'll miss her."

"I'm sorry, Lake. I'll miss her too."

"Such a faithful friend. I wish I could love as she did and be as faithful to people as she was. I mean, I know she's a dog, but she was more Christ like than I am. She had unconditional love. She'd kiss a burglar!"

"Lake..."

"I know it sounds weird. Life is so hard, Kenzie. But God is so good, and the best is yet to come. I want him to reign in us, Kenzie. As much as he rained on me today, I want him to reign in me."

"Let's pray that, Lake. God, as you rained today on your creation, reign in us, your servants. Flood us with your presence."

"Rain, reign. Hmmmm," Lake pondered. "A beautiful day, Kenzie. A beautiful night. Let's go back to the cabin."

A week later, Lake received Sheba's ashes. He ran the five miles to the knoll to spread them on the grass and placed some into the lake because she loved to swim. After he was done, he prayed and slowly walked away from the knoll. Leaving under a beautiful sunset Lake looked back at the knoll.

Trembling, he shouted, "You be a good girl, Sheba. I love you!" Slowly, he turned and ran down the hill and disappeared in the forest.

7

The Downward Spiral:
A Stronghold in Times of Trouble

Lake was having coffee and cleaning at the Eddy when Brisk, Lawrence, and Parker arrived. Brisk gave Lake a quick kiss, a gentle hug, and asked, "Are you ready?"

"Where are you going again?" Lawrence yelled across the room. "Why are you dressed up? I never thought you had any dress clothes. Maybe you should drive Parker's grocery-getter, and I'll take the Jeep."

Lake replied, "Not a chance with the Jeep. Some friends of Brisk had extra tickets to a seminar on the History of Jerusalem up at the North Mountain Christian Center, so she asked me to go. Even though she doesn't like history, she knows I love it. I think it will be interesting. Shirt and tie required, I had to think about that part.

"See you later, Lawrence. See ya, Parker."

"Catch you, guys, tonight," Lawrence replied. Parker smiled and gave a military salute.

After getting in the Jeep and buckling up, Lake looked at Brisk and said, "You look so beautiful in that dress, all those blue and white flowers, especially the blue. Do you want the top on the Jeep?"

"No way! It's a beautiful day!" she said. "I didn't have to think about what color to wear. You look handsome in blue, Lake. Where'd you get the clothes? I never thought you had any dress clothes either."

"Don't any of you MacCabees think I have any class? And I'm not handsome!" he said, laughing. Then his smile faded. "I used to be a manager at one job and had to dress up. I hated that part. After a year, the boss left me go. I was the only guy on her staff, and I think she resented it. My people liked me, and I think she resented that too and the fact my group improved the most. Before she left me go, she said the reason was because I was unable to give negative feedback to my people. But that's why my people improved. I encouraged them and gave positive feedback. I guess it was more important to follow the rules than to help people achieved their potential. I'm rambling, I'm sorry. I didn't sleep well last night, as usual. I'm just tired. Let's talk about something else."

"You are good at encouraging people. Look, you got all us to run with you and you helped every one of us with our music. You even bought little Parker his first guitar," she told him.

"Look at the mountains," Lake responded, trying to change the subject. "They are so beautiful this time of year."

Brisk shook her head and just smiled.

The two-hour drive through the mountains was relaxing and beautiful. Brisk and Lake talked, sang, and prayed all the way. North Mountain Christian Center was in a remote section of the state. Pulling onto the parking lot, Lake and Brisk looked around in amazement at the natural beauty that surrounded the campus and how the center was able to preserve it amongst the buildings.

They found their way to the auditorium, met Brisk's friends, and found their seats. Lake was filling out his registration form and did not look up when the instructor was introduced. He applauded politely with the others while keeping focus on the forms. Brisk nudged him with her elbow and whispered, "Pay attention." He smiled and winked at her then looked forward. Then his face turned white. For a moment, his breathing stopped and he appeared frozen. His pen slowly rolled from his hand and onto the floor. Brisk retrieved the pen and handed it to Lake. He didn't respond. She said, "Lake! Lake! What's wrong?" Again, no response.

Suddenly, he got up and bolted out toward the back of the auditorium. Brisk followed. Once outside, he immediately sat on the grass, head in his knees. Brisk knelt behind him and placed her arms around him. "What's wrong, what happened?" she said but he was silent. "Lake, we're missing the class. What can I do?"

"I don't feel good. Please just go in, and I'll join you if I feel better but I doubt it. I need some air. I just need some air. I'm sorry."

Brisk began to pray, "Lord God, help Lake whatever it is that is bothering him. In Jesus's name."

She kissed Lake on the neck and hesitantly walked back inside, stopping to look back as the door closed.

The class lasted several hours. Brisk came out and found Lake sitting against a tree in front of his Jeep. He had changed from his dress clothes into shorts and a tank top. Brisk said harshly, "What was your problem?"

Lake replied, "Are you ready to go?"

"You embarrassed me in front of my friends," she said. "They think you're a little weird. What happened? You were all excited about today, then, all of a sudden, you looked like you saw the face of death. What happened?"

"I just want to go home. Are you ready to go?" Lake said, not being able to look at her.

They got into the Jeep and began to head home. Just as Lake turned on the radio, Brisk turned it off. After an hour of silence, Brisk began asking questions again. Calmly, she asked, "Lake, what is wrong?" She reached over with her hand to brush Lake's hair from his brow. He quickly tilted his head away from her.

With a long sigh, she sat back in her seat and said, "I can't figure you out. Can't you say anything?"

While she talked, Lake was observing the mountain ridge to his left. He said, "It's going to be a beautiful full moon night."

"What frequency are you on?" Brisk said angrily. "Can't you talk to me? Can't you explain what happened today?"

Slowly, Lake said, "My spirit is greatly distressed. It's beyond explanation. Sometimes only God can be the counselor."

"What are you trying to say? There's a disturbance in the force?" she said sarcastically. "I'm starting to think you are weird."

Lake pulled into a gravel parking lot about 6:00 p.m. It was the trailhead for the Escarpment Trail. He jumped out and dialed a number on his cell phone while he walked over to Brisk's side of the jeep so she could hear. "Kenzie! Brisk is taking my jeep home tonight. She'll pick you up at 8:00 a.m. for breakfast. She has a lot of questions and you have full freedom to answer anything she asks. Yes. I'm sure. I'm doing an overnight run up Escarpment Trail tonight. Yup, all thirty miles, not a problem. Hope to be at North Point about midnight. Well thanks. I've been hearing that 'W' word a lot today. Can you meet her? Good. See you at church. Bye!"

While lifting his hydration pack out of the back of the Jeep he says, "Brisk. Meet Kenzie tomorrow morning at eight at the cabin. He'll tell you what I can't tell you. I need lake time. I need to be alone with God tonight. Please understand."

"Yes, sir," she said with a salute. "Lake, I don't know what to think. You have this mysterious side to you that worries me. I'm trying to understand, but it is making me angry. If you can't open up to me, who can you open up to?"

"I open up to God. He understands. He comforts me. I'm not sure you'd understand," he said.

Angrily, she replied, "What I don't understand is why your Jeep was at Marilyn Smith's house overnight last week. Mrs. Mahoosic told me. You know what Marilyn's reputation is and why Lawrence broke off their engagement. I just was keeping it to myself, hoping there was a good explanation. You being there with her, that's what I don't understand."

"It's not what you think," he said while looking at the ground. "Just because she went out with a guy with a bad reputation doesn't make her bad. You all found her guilty by association. Lawrence wouldn't listen to a word she said."

With her left hand, she pulls up Lake's chin, trying to get him to look at her but he looks around her. With that, she slapped him with her right hand. "You're a typical man!" she snapped.

"No I'm not, I mean, yes, I am, and I mean… You don't understand. You don't know!" She slapped him again. Stepping back, he yelled, "Stop hitting me! If I wanted to get slapped around, I'd go to a family reunion! Now stop it!"

After a few minutes of silence, Lake said, "Brisk. We've been friends for almost a year. I like you very much. But some things we are handed in life are difficult to deal with. Some scars never heal. We just hide them with a Band-Aid. Then, when everything seems to be okay for years, the Band-Aid is ripped off and the scar appears. I just need time to myself. Please understand. Please trust me."

As she walked around the Jeep to the driver's seat, Brisk said, "Trust you? You don't trust me with whatever is bothering you. And like? You like me. That's all you can say? Well, I loved you! You can't even say the word." Then she hit the gas hard, spraying Lake with gravel.

"I don't know what love is," Lake said while watching the Jeep disappear into the distance. "Guess I lost another one." He turned to look at the mountains, placed his pack on, and began slowly walking up the trail. After a few miles of slow walking and deep thinking, he came to a bridge. Leaning over the railing and looking into the water, he silently prayed. The tears began to flow. As each one hit the water, small pools of ripples migrated outward. Then he saw the beautiful reflection of the moon in the water. He stood and smiled as he watched the moon rising over the ridge. He raised his hands and said, "Thank you, Jesus. You're running with me tonight. Thank you." He turned and began running up the trail.

At Mirror Pond, Lake stopped. Taking off his pack and undressing, he walked into the pond, then swam into the middle. Finding some footing, he stood completely still. On the west were the remains of an orange, pink, and purple sunset. To the east, a beautiful full moon was rising. Lake whispered, "Thank you, God, for your creativity. No sunset is ever the same. No moonrise is ever the same. You are so beautiful." Lake stood completely still, just listening. Coyotes began howling on the east shore. Their loud howls and snarls echoed throughout the forest. Just as quickly as they started, they were silent. A whip-poor-will to the north was calling out its repetitious song. To the south, another was answering. Crickets and frogs called out along the shoreline. The water was now still. The stars were appearing in the sky and in reflections on the water. "God, you are so beautiful. Thank you for this moment."

Lake swan to the shore, and he put on his pack. He sang as he cautiously ran the trail in the moonlight. Some areas of thick forest required a headlamp but along the rocky edge of the escarpment the moonlight was sufficient. North Point allowed a 360-degree view. He arrived just before midnight. Lake dropped his pack. The katydids were chanting in the trees below the cliffs. The moon reflected off Lake's sweating body.

He knelt and prayed. Then standing, he proclaimed, "You reign forever! You have established your throne for judgment! You will judge the world in righteousness! You will govern us with justice! You are a refuge for the oppressed, a stronghold in times of trouble! Those who know your name will trust in you, for you, Lord, have never forsaken those who seek you!"

After taking in the moonlit night and the awesome views, Lake pulled out an emergency blanket from his pack. He curled up in the blanket and, rolling onto his back, gazed at the moon and the stars. "Father God, I love you."

Lake woke at 3:00 a.m., shivering from the morning cold and the dew. Still wrapped in the blanket he rose to his knees and said, "Thank you, God, for a beautiful morning. That's so cool how you filled those valleys with the fog. The moon is shining on everything! Thank you for letting me see this! Thank you!"

He took a drink from the hydration system in his pack and ate an energy bar. After taking in the view one last time, he cuffed his hands around his mouth and left go his imitation of a coyote howl. Then he laughed and begin a slow careful run across the rocks and then down into the woods. At 4:30 a.m., Lake crossed the last bridge and he came to the highway that led five miles to his cabin. It was getting light out, and he was enjoying the early morning bird songs and the dew on the wildflowers. Lake was on his porch at 5:15 a.m., watching the sunrise.

Looking toward the sun, he wearily prayed, "Thank you, God, for a beautiful night. Thank you for safety. Please bring Brisk back to me. Please forgive me. Thank you, Lord. You are amazing. Today is going to be better day. Going to sleep."

Lake went in the house, got a shower, set the alarm for eight, and fell asleep.

Kenzie peeked in Lake's room at seven thirty to make sure he made it home. Brisk came by to drop off Lake's Jeep. After a short discussion, they got in Kenzie's Jeep and left for town. Lake slept so sound the music alarm failed to wake him up when it went off. He woke about ten thirty and jumped up when he saw the time on his clock. He threw a frozen breakfast meal into the microwave and then took another quick shower. Getting out of the shower, he did a balancing act of trying to get dried off, dressed, and attempting to eat his breakfast all at the same time. Grabbing his Bible off the table, he began to run out the door but then slowed to a walk saying to himself, "Oh, these legs are a little sore today."

Lake was going to miss most of church, but he always wanted to be there. When he arrived, he saw Lawrence, Brandy, Zachariah, and Parker sitting on a pile of railroad ties at the end of the parking lot. He pulled in beside them and said, "What are you guys doing out here?" At first, no one said a word. Then Zachariah finally spoke up. He said, "Remember how Pastor Avalon, that new associate pastor, or ass pastor for short, kept cutting back the worship time? Well, today he told us that while he's here there will be no music from Lucifer's Lot. He said our music was of the devil! So we sat there while he sang some soulish solo. Halfway through, we couldn't stand it and we came out here. A few other people came out behind us and left."

"First, don't speak badly about God's anointed, ever if you are in doubt. Second, you all do a wonderful job leading worship. You don't try to please anyone. You strive to listen to and please only the Lord, and everyone knows that. Your hearts are right. Hey, he's only here for a few weeks filling in for Pastor Bentley, maybe we can endure until then."

"Pastor Bentley is here today. He's back for just this weekend. Maybe you could talk to him," Zachariah half pleaded.

"Where is Brisk and Kenzie? I thought they'd be here by now," Lake asked.

Zachariah replied, "They called and said they had a meeting that was taking longer than planned. They felt bad they were missing church, but believe me, they didn't miss anything."

"Wait here for me," Lake said. "I'll go in and catch the rest of the service and maybe talk to Bentley. But who am I that anyone would listen. Pray!"

Lake went in and sat five rows back on the right side. After ten minutes of listening to Pastor Avalon glorify himself, Lake's spirit was so grieved he knew he had to say something. While Pastor Avalon was looking toward the opposite side of the room, Lake quickly scooted up to the front and slid down the pew where Pastor Bentley was sitting, bumping into him.

"What are you doing?" Pastor Bentley whispered.

"Sir, this guy kicked the worship team out this morning, really demoralizing them. Said they were Lucifer's Lot. Now I'm listening to him talk about how a wonderful Christian he is. Of course, that's what he talked about last week, the week before, and the week before that. Must be some series or something. You got to do something."

Pastor Bentley said, "Well, Lake, that's the most I ever heard you talk in church. I thought you and Parker were in a who-can-talk-the-least competition. Anyway, I know there is a problem, that's why I came back this weekend, to see what was going on. But I promised him complete authority over the church while I was away. My hands are tied."

"Well, sir, mine aren't," Lake replied.

"I know you won't make a scene, right?"

Lake smiled and shook his head. "I guess I couldn't if I wanted to. I'm going back to my seat and politely suffer through the rest of the, ah, sermon."

Lake got up and began walking back to his seat. Pastor Avalon stopped talking and said, "Excuse me, young man, do you have a problem?"

Lake turned around and pointing to himself said, "Me?"

"Yeah, you, the hippie."

Looking toward Pastor Bentley, Lake mouths, "He started it." Turning back toward Pastor Avalon, he continued, "Ah, no problem, sir. I just had a question."

"Why don't you ask me the question since I'm the one in charge here?"

"Well, the question is, are you preaching, pretending, or performing?"

"What on Earth do you mean?"

"Well, since I've been sitting here, trying to stay awake, all I've heard is about is you. Not once, not once did you mention the name of Jesus Christ. Don't you know that it's all about him?"

Pastor Bentley had his hand over his face as Pastor Avalon replied to Lake's charges. "Let me explain. There are glorified Christians, like myself, who are able to enjoy our years of maturing to perfection. Then there are Christians, ones like yourself, if you are indeed a Christian, who will never mature to our level. We're here to lead you, the weak."

"Sir, I am a Christian," Lake replied.

"I'm sorry, son. I certainly couldn't tell by looking at you."

Lake turned to Pastor Bentley, who still has his hand over his face, and said to him, "This can't be real. Are we on *Candid Camera* or something?" Lake grabbed his Bible and walked toward the back of the church. He stopped when he heard Pastor Avalon say, "Pray for this unsaved hippie mountain boy. He needs the Lord." Lake briefly closed his eyes, took a deep breath, and then walked outside.

Outside, Lake shook his head, and said, "God, I'm sorry, but this one's a jerk. But he's your problem, you deal with him, I've got enough problem of my own. What's a hippie?"

"You're the hippie," Justin told him as he stood by the exit. "You know what, Nid-has-been? I should be the one up there, not Avalon."

"Well, Justin," Lake began, "I can't believe I'm saying this, but you could do a better job than Avalon. You both are kind of similar, though."

"What do you mean, Nid-has-been?"

"That's Nidhatak. Well, both of you are in love with yourselves and you think you are better than everyone. But to be a leader, you must start as a servant."

"Shut up. I am born a leader!"

"No. Like Avalon you were born a performer. You both are trying for acceptance and love. Just humble yourself before the Lord and—"

"Shut up and get out of my church. You better watch your back, man. I've got a target on it."

"Justin, are you still mad about me kicking you out of the Eddy? You came out singing, sliding across the stage, and displayed a sickening soulish performance. It was terrible and I'm not sorry I told you to leave. You were affecting everyone! Some felt disturbed in spirit, and others outright laughed at you."

"You embarrassed me, and I'll never forgive you!"

"Justin, I always told you that you can return if you humble yourself. You have a great voice, but you always want to be the star of the show. It's not about you Justin. It's about Jesus."

Justin grabbed Lake's neck and pushed him into the wall. "Don't try to preach to me, Nid-has-been, 'cause I'll kill you!"

Lake broke free and slammed Justin against the wall. "Don't you ever threaten me, Mackenzie, or any of the Judah Lion bandmembers ever, never, ever. Do you hear me, Justin?" Justin was silent. "Justin, if you want to be a leader you have to start as a servant. You have to humble yourself. Justin, I mean that as a friend."

Lake left Justin go but Justin took a swing at Lake and Lake ducked.

"Oh, Justin. You missed!"

"I won't miss next time. I swear I won't miss next time!"

"Have a good day, Justin!" Lake said as he walked toward the parking lot.

Walking over to the band he tried to encourage the team. "Hey, this guy can't be for real. Don't listen to whatever he has to say about you. You know the Truth and you know how to be lead worshipers. Remember a few weeks ago at practice, each one of you were on your knees at the alter: Kenzie holding up his drum sticks, Brandy holding up her violin, Parker holding up his saxophone, Brisk holding her clarinet, Lawrence and Zachariah, holding your guitars above your heads. Every one of you surrendering your will to the Lord. I don't know where this guy came from or what Bible he reads, but he is definitely one fry short of a happy meal. Not only is his waistline supersized but so is his ego."

Church was over, and people were walking to their cars. Lake paid no attention but kept his focus on the band even as people walked past them. "In a race," he continues, "if something trips you and you fall, you don't just lay there and wonder why. You don't lick your wounds. You get up and keep on running. You don't even think about it. When the race is over, you may remember that fall, laugh at it, and brag about the wounds suffered but you still kept on going and you finished. So don't let this guy mess with your ministry. Either play right here, or let's invite everyone to the Eddy and play there." Several bystanders applauded Lake. "Preach it, brother!" one yelled.

Another said, "You should be in there preaching! We're not coming back until he's gone!"

An embarrassed Lake turned and responded, "Just pray for him, please, just pray for him.

"Lake! Lake!" yelled Pastor Bentley from the side door. "Kenzie has been trying to reach you on your cell phone but got no answer. He's on the office phone. Says it is urgent."

Lake reached for his cell phone then said, "Oh, must have left it at home. I'll be back, guys." As he turned toward the church, he bumped into Mrs. Mahoosic. "I'm sorry, Mrs. Mahoosic, please excuse me," he said to her.

"You certainly are sorry. You're trash," she snipped.

"What? What do you mean?" Lake asked, smiling. "Where you talking to my dad again?" She stuck her head into the air and turned away from him. "I'm sorry, I didn't mean to bump into you. It was an accident, Mrs. Mahoosic. I am trash…redeemed trash!"

"Lake!" Pastor Bentley yelled once again from the door.

"Yes, sir," Lake responded and ran toward the church.

Inside Pastor Bentley said, "Take the call here in Pastor Avalon's office, its closer. In the office, Pastor Bentley picked up the phone. "Kenzie? Here's Lake."

While handing the phone to Lake, Pastor Avalon, sitting in his new mahogany chair, protested. "Hey, I do not allow those type of people in my office. He can't touch my furniture and especially not my phone!"

Pastor Bentley pleaded, "Pastor Avalon, please be silent. This call is important."

"What's the matter, Kenzie?" Lake asked. "When? What happened? Where are you at? Meet you at the cabin." Lake, staring at the floor, handed the phone back to Pastor Bentley. Pastor Bentley turned around and began talking to Kenzie privately.

"Kenzie?" Pastor Avalon says with a chuckle. "That's that other long-haired hippie mountain boy. I saw you two hugging two weeks ago Sunday up on Otter Lake Road. I didn't think they left your type of people in this church."

Lake quickly turned and faced Avalon. "What do you mean 'your type of people'?" he angrily asked.

Pastor Avalon stood up, smiling behind his desk, and said, "Queers. You and that Kenzie, queers."

"What?" Lake yelled and walked toward the desk.

Pastor Bentley turned, placed his hand over the receiver, and said, "You guys stop it right now!"

Lake took his left arm and pulled everything off Pastor Avalon's desk. Avalon said confidently, "You're nothing but a little punk."

With a swing from his right arm, Lake punched Pastor Avalon, knocking him to the floor. "Listen to me, you white-washed sepulcher," Lake screamed. "I'm Lakeland Nidhatak! Kenzie is Mackenzie Nidhatak! He's my brother! My flesh and blood brother! Otter Lake Road is where my father lives! Two weeks ago, my father beat the hell out of Kenzie, and I went there to rescue him. He was a bloody mess, that's why I was holding him. I can't believe you would be misjudging that terrible day. How could you miss the blood on him? Apparently, you never read about the Good Samaritan! You just drove by judging!" Lake stood there, trembling as he looked at

Avalon. Pastor Avalon sat on the floor holding his chin, looking back at Lake with no expression.

"By the way, since no one else here has the courage, I'll say it… you're fired!" Lake yelled at the top of his voice. He turned and began walking out the door.

"Lake!" Pastor Bentley said, trying to stop him.

"Don't 'Lake' me, Pastor Prosperity and Popularity. When are *you* going to start preaching the Word? You read one or two scriptures a week and you call that a sermon? Look at your people! They are starving! Look at the service today, has anyone been changed? Has anyone been saved? We want to hear about donkeys that talk, gourds that shade prophets, giants that are slain, a queen that saves her people, a kinsman redeemer, and a God with such a great love gave his Son for us. Wake up and check the hour! We have no more time to waste! Your sheep are scattered!"

"Because of people like you," as he pointed to Pastor Avalon, "and people like you," as he pointed at Bentley, "I give up Christianity! I'm going to follow Yahshua!" Lake turned and walked out.

"I'll be in touch, Kenzie," Pastor Bentley says softly on the phone. "The Lord is with you. Goodbye."

"Pastor Avalon, that was Kenzie, you know, Lake's brother? It was an emergency phone call that's why I asked Lake to come here instead of going all the way to my office. Their father passed away about an hour ago." Pastor Bentley turned and walked to the door. Looking back at Pastor Avalon, still on the floor, he said, "I wished I had some of Lake's courage because I'd punch you again. And by the way, you're fired!"

As Lake stormed out of the church, he ran into Mrs. Mahoosic again. She began saying, "Oh, Lakeland! You're so bad. I heard you and Brisk broke up, all because you were sleeping with that Smith girl. I also heard—"

Lake interrupted her. "Mrs. Mahoosic, Mr. Avalon and Mr. Fist just met head on in the church because of misinformation on his part. I don't know where you get your misinformation, but I'm tired of it! You are a distraction and a disgrace to this to this body of Christ, and it is beyond me why no one has ever brought that to your attention!"

"If I ever hear you gossip about Mackenzie or Brisk, or anyone else, Mr. Fist is going to reach down your throat and pull your poisonous tongue out. Haven't you read that death and life are in the power of the tongue? Are you speaking death or life?"

"If I were you, I'd go in the church, bow down at the altar, and ask God for forgiveness. Ask him for a new tongue. Then, next Sunday, stand up before this church and testify how he has changed you. So get in there. Right now!" She began slowly walking toward the church but stopped to look back. "Get in there!" Lake yelled. She turned and began walking faster. "Mrs. Mahoosic," Lake yelled, "I'll be praying for you. God changes people. He loves you!" With tears in her eyes, she turned and went inside.

Lake walked over to the band. "Hey, something bad has happened. Please, let's go to Eddy or anywhere to talk and pray. I really need your help today, guys. Come on, let's go somewhere, anywhere except church."

Lawrence walked in front of Lake and stopped him while Parker walked behind Lake. "Mrs. Mahoosic has informed us of your extra-curricular activities." Parker grabbed Lake's arms and pulled them behind his back. Lawrence punched Lake in the stomach then again in the face. Brandy and Zachariah rushed in to stop it. After the scuffle, they stood alongside Lawrence and Parker facing Lake. In pain, Lake barely got out, "What are you doing? What's going on?"

"That's for cheating on our sister."

"I didn't cheat on your sister!"

"Mrs. Mahoosic said your Jeep was at Marilyn Smith's house overnight last week. She said you dumped Brisk. You know what? She's right, you're trash. You always tell us about your father saying that you'll never amount to anything. Well, he was right too."

Brandy interrupted, "Lawrence, that's enough."

But Lawrence continued, "Forget about the race. Why should we run under the church name when they kicked us out? Forget about the worship band. We would have made a lot of money if we'd had stayed on the club circuit. But we listened to you and here we are broke sitting on pile of old, useless railroad ties. Useless! We thought you were helping us, but you left us down, big time. You are no longer our so-called spiritual advisor. You're done. You're just a big dreaming worthless punk."

Lake grabbed Lawrence and slammed him up against Lawrence's van. All was quiet. While holding Lawrence firm against the van, Lake looked at each one of them. He softly said, "Are all of you in agreement with what Lawrence said?" but no one replied. He screamed, "Are all you in agreement with what Lawrence said?" No one made a sound. Lake looked intensely at a frightful Lawrence for a minute then released him. "Enemies hurt. Friends kill," Lake told him. Then he turned and walked to his Jeep and without looking back drove away.

"What did he mean by 'Enemies hurt. Friends kill?'" Brandy asked.

"One of his stupid sayings," Lawrence replied.

"But they usually make sense, eventually. Like the one 'Friends are like leaves on a tree. They change with the seasons. When things get cold, they dry up and float away. But occasionally, you find an evergreen.' He said we were his evergreen friends. I wonder what he's thinking now."

"I think we really made a big mistake, Lawrence," Zachariah said.

"Shut up! Just shut up. He's weird," Lawrence shot back.

"Yeah, he's weird. But who else has ever stood behind us? Who else has ever pushed us to do our best, to live for God, to follow our dreams? I think you may have overdone it, Lawrence," Zachariah told him.

"No. He over did it by the way he treated my sister. Shut up, he'll get over it."

Brandy added, "Maybe it's not true. Maybe we shouldn't be judging him. After all, it came from Mrs. Mahoosic." Parker stood there, hands in his pockets, looking downward, scratching the ground with his foot.

Marilyn Smith was walking toward them and caught their attention. "Hi, everyone. Hi, Lawrence," she said. Lawrence looked away.

"I was hoping to hear you sing in church today. Lake said you had an excellent worship band going. I wasn't sure if I'd make it this week. I saw Lake come in late but didn't get to talk to him. Where is he?"

"He just left. Why were *you* in church?" Lawrence asked.

"I ran into Lake last week, and we talked and talked all night. He talked about each one of you, how God has gifted you with your music. He talked, of course, about running. He said you were his best friend, Lawrence. But best of all, he told me about Jesus. He told me how much Jesus loves me. We knelt and prayed early in the morning. Lake insisted on going outside, under the stars and a half moon. It was a beautiful night. I gave my heart to Jesus. That's why I'm in church today. Oh, congratulations on your big break!"

"What do you mean big break?" Lawrence asked.

"You being selected to play at the county fair."

"What are you talking about?"

"Lake said he knew some officials up there and pulled some strings. He strongly suggested your band's name to do all the music one night. He said there are several thousand people there plus TV coverage."

"He didn't say anything to us," Zachariah said.

"Oh, dear," she said. "He was going to tell you at the Eddy last night. I thought you'd know. I'm sorry."

"He didn't show up last night. He was on one of his crazy runs," Lawrence answered.

The band's eyes were fixed on him. "What are you looking at? Okay, okay! I screwed up. Oh, man, I screwed up big time. What am I going to do now? Marilyn, no need for you to say you're sorry. I'm the one who needs to say I'm sorry to you and to Lake." He walked over and gave her a hug. "Welcome. I'm so happy for you. I truly am." Everyone took a turn embracing her.

Pastor Bentley walked over to the group. "Lake. Where's Lake?"

"What's wrong?" Brandy asked.

"Well, he left very upset. He punched Pastor Avalon. I think we better find him," he said.

"What was the phone call from Kenzie about? You said it was urgent," she asked.

"Their father passed away this morning. I think that set off a downward spiral. He kind of lost it in there. Said to Kenzie he'd meet him at the cabin."

"Oh, man, in his time of need we, I mean I, left him down big time. Let's go to his cabin," Lawrence said to the band. "Pastor, we'll give you a call when we find him. Marilyn, I'll call you. Good seeing you again. We'll talk. Okay! Let's go!" The band loaded up into Lawrence's van and headed toward Lake's cabin.

8

Lost Lake

Lake had arrived home. He walked into his study and looked around. He stared at an old picture of his parents and three little boys. Then he picked up one of his guitars and smashed it over his computer stand, breaking his trophies and many pictures. A picture of band hanging on the wall caught his attention. He walked over and touched the face of each one, praying silently. He went to punch the picture but stopped himself. Then, seeing his backpack, he picked it up and went to the studio. There he placed another guitar inside the best he could, half sticking out. He headed outside and placed the pack in his Jeep. Walking to the porch, he grabbed his mountain bike and placed it on the Jeep. As he started to get into the Jeep, he stopped and looked around. "Help me hold it together, God," he said. "Big boys don't cry. Big boys don't cry. Big boys don't cry." Then he left.

The band arrived about ten minutes after Lake left. Kenzie and Brisk were already there. As the group walked up to the front door, they came out.

"Is there anything we can do for you, Mackenzie?" Brandy asked as she gave him a hug.

"Find my brother," a sad Kenzie replied. "He smashed his guitar over his trophies. He left a real mess. I think we need to find him. There's more going on in his head than you could imagine."

"He punched Pastor Avalon at church and threatened Mrs. Mahoosic," Zachariah said.

"What?" Kenzie said, startled. "He's never been violent, until today, and that's not good. Now I'm really worried."

"That's not all, Kenzie. Um, Mrs. Mahoosic told us Lake was at Marilyn Smith's house overnight last week. I thought the worst, and when Lake came out of the church, I belted him. One in the face and one in the stomach."

"You did what?" Kenzie yelled as he shoved Lawrence. "You are supposed to be his friend!"

"I had no idea he had gotten your phone call about your father. That's when he left. I feel so terrible."

"You should," Kenzie snipped.

"Here he led Marilyn to the Lord, that's why he was at her house," Lawrence told them.

"Are you serious, Lawrence? That's why he was there, not because…" Brisk asked.

"He led her to the Lord that night. I don't know if he can ever forgive me," Lawrence replied.

"How can he forgive me?" Brisk replied. "I really let him have it last night, I was so upset. God forgive me."

"Where do you think he went?" Lawrence asked.

"Where do you think? Where does he go to pray? Where do we always have to stop when running or biking to pray?" Kenzie said to refresh their minds.

"The knoll!" Zachariah shouted.

"The knoll," Lawrence whispers.

"The knoll, of course," said Brandy.

"Lawrence, I'm sorry. You are a good friend to Lake and me. We'll get this all straightened out. Everyone, grab some bikes, it's seven miles out there," Kenzie suggested. "Lawrence, I think once you explain everything, he'll understand. I hope."

"I hope so too. But I won't blame him if he never talks to me again. I really left him down. If only he'd tell me stuff like going to Marilyn's."

"He probably wanted Marilyn to give you the good news. You know he likes others to tell good news or be in the limelight. He wants to be a nameless hero. He thinks differently that we do, really differently," Kenzie said as he placed his hand on Lawrence's shoulder. "We'll get it all straightened out. Let's go."

A half hour later, Lawrence's van and Kenzie's Jeep pulled into the parking lot beside the gate to the game lands. Lake's Jeep was parked nearby. Lawrence, Parker, and Zachariah jumped out of the van and immediately got their bikes and packs ready. Kenzie, Brisk, and Brandy got out of the Kenzie's Jeep. "I'm taking my recorder," Brisk yelled over to Lawrence. "I'm taking my guitar! We're thinking the same thing! He's out there worshiping. Knowing him, he's expecting us!"

They began to bike, but just pass the gate Lawrence hit his back brake and slid sideways to a halt in front of everyone. Everyone stopped. "Hey, what would Lake do right now, before we'd go anywhere?"

"Pray!" Zachariah said with a smile.

"Father," Lawrence began, "thank you for this beautiful day. Forgive us. Forgive me. Let Lake be safe. Give peace to him. We thank you for him. He's weird but he sure knows how to have fun in life. In Jesus's name. Amen."

"And what does he make us yell?" he asked.

"Blessed be your name today, Lord God!" they all shouted together.

"Look! A squirrel!" Zachariah said, mimicking what Lake always did before a run. Everyone briefly laughed then all were quiet, everyone in deep thought. "Let's go," Kenzie yelled. "To the knoll!"

"To the knoll," each one yelled.

Forty minutes later, the fast line of six mountain bikes arrived at the road to the knoll. Getting off their bikes, Lawrence said, "This guitar weighs a ton!"

"It's so beautiful here," Brisk exclaimed. "No wonder he comes here all the time." They began walking together up the first small hill. On top of the hill, the knoll was in full view as well as the whole lake and small islands. Everyone stopped and looked, their faces in sheer disappointment.

"He's not here," Brisk said as she started to cry.

Everyone stared at the knoll.

"He wasn't expecting us. He doesn't want us," Lawrence whispered. "What have I done to my friend, our brother?"

For a few minutes, all that could be heard was the warm breeze passing through the trees. Then Lawrence spoke up, "Let's walk out to the knoll. Let's, ah, go out and, ah, pray. See what God wants us to do."

They began walking the grass road atop the earthen dam to the knoll. Brandy and Kenzie walked ahead, hand in hand. Lawrence and Brisk were just behind them. Lawrence had his arm around Brisk's shoulders. Parker and Zachariah waded in the water along the shoreline, parallel to the others.

Arriving at the top of the knoll, Lawrence said, "Okay, everyone, let's join hands and pray." Lawrence, Brisk, Kenzie, and Brandy joined hands but left an open space for Parker and Zachariah. "Hurry up, you guys!" Kenzie yelled. As they were waiting, Brandy said, "Lawrence, I'm amazed at you taking the lead to pray. That's twice today."

"Well, I had a good teacher," he replied and then turned to look out across the pond to gain his composure. Parker and Zachariah joined the group. "Okay, everyone," Lawrence began. "Father. I don't know what to say right now. I don't have big fancy words to impress you or anyone listening like they do in church. All I know is that you know our hearts. All I have is a simple request: help us find Lake. Thank you."

Brisk began playing her recorder. Lawrence joined in with his guitar. Kenzie and Brandy found some sticks and started tapping them together. Zachariah stood there humming along, eyes closed, facing the pond. Parker was lying on his side among the buttercups down by the edge of the pond. He was studying a map of the game lands and tapping his foot to the music. A flock of geese flew by low and landed in the water nearby, as if enjoying what they were hearing.

When the music stopped, Brisk turned toward Kenzie and said, "Kenzie, can I talk to you privately for a few minutes?"

"Sure," he responded. They walked over to the outlet from the pond. "Lawrence said the last thing Lake told him was 'Enemies hurt. Friends kill.' What do you think he meant by that? He's not going to hurt himself, is he?"

"No, no. Of course not. He's beyond that," he said.

"What do you mean by 'beyond that'?" she asked.

"Brisk, let me explain. First, the phrase simply means while enemies can make you feel bad or hurt your feelings. It is, according to him, friends and family who really do the wounding. Think about it. It's kind of true. Especially after what I told you this morning, he is justified in that statement. The people he trusted the most were the ones who have hurt him the most. I think we all can say that's true even in our lives."

"Second, what I meant by 'beyond that' is that he is beyond suicide or hurting himself in anyway. He tried that several times, he told me. After those events, I told you about this morning he decided even God didn't like him. But after the last attempt, he woke up and felt different. He said he was going to make it and nothing is going to bring him down ever again. He knew it was providence."

"So what do you think is going on with him?" Brisk asked.

"I think he simply needs to be alone. He is disappointed with people, maybe, but not bitter. When we find him, he'll probably act as if nothing ever happened, even though he is hurting inside. He seldom expresses how he feels if he thinks it will upset anyone. I think he needs to review his relationship with our dad. I think there is a lot he needs to run through his head. I hate to say it, but our dad's death may be a release for him. It's almost terrible to say but I think it is true. I'm sorry, I shouldn't have said that."

Brisk hugged Kenzie and he began to cry. "Brisk, why is life so hard!"

"It's okay to cry, Kenzie. You haven't yet since you found out about your father. You got to let it out," she said.

With tears in his eyes and a slight smile, Kenzie reminded Brisk, "Hey, I'm the psychology major!"

As he continued to cry, he said, "Brisk, I always thought you and Lake were a perfect match. You got to reach into him. He has no value for himself. He needs you. Don't let him drive you away. He doesn't mean to, it's just hard for him to accept anyone likes him. Give him time. Please."

"Don't worry, Kenzie. I don't give up easy!" she said while wiping the tears from his eyes with a tissue. "I wonder if he can forgive me for slapping him. I never slapped anyone, Kenzie. I just care so much for him and the thought of him with Marilyn…"

"I don't know what to say, Brisk. He's hurting, hurting really bad. I always wondered how long he'd keep it to himself."

After a few quiet minutes, Brisk said to Kenzie, "Come on. Let's find out what we are going to do." They begin walking back to the others. "Remember Lake's phrase, Kenzie, 'Life is hard, but God is good…'"

"And the best is yet to come," Kenzie added with a smile.

Lawrence walked down to Parker and said to him, "You know, Lake always said the moon came up late here because of that hill to the east. I'm thinking he went to another pond out here. We never went with him because, um, because we thought he was nuts! I vaguely remember him mentioning a place where he could see the moon come up and the sun set at the same time. So it had to be a vastly level area, at least on the east and the west. But which of the hundreds of ponds in these one hundred thousand acres of wilderness could it be?"

Parker sat up. He took his index finger and hit a point on the map hard.

"Mirror Pond? Up there on Escarpment Trail?" he asked Parker. Parker nodded his head.

"We've never been out there. That's going to take about, what, three hours? Can you lead the way?"

Parker nodded in affirmation and with a big smile. He stood up, placed two fingers in his mouth, and then left out an ear-piercing whistle. Kenzie, Brisk, Brandy, and Zachariah looked in his direction. With his hand, he signaled for them to follow. They walked quickly across the dam to the bikes.

At the bikes, Lawrence briefed them on the plan for the evening. "Listen, everyone," he began. "Parker suspects, and I agree, that Lake is out at Mirror Pond on Escarpment Trail."

"That's where he was last night," Brisk told them.

"Right," Lawrence replied. "He probably wants to be with his other friends he runs with at night so we need to find him and prove we are his friends too. We aren't going to let him down when he needs us most."

"What other running friends?" Brandy asked.

The guys looked at each other and then began laughing.

"What's so funny?" Brisk asked. "What other friends?"

"You never heard him talk about the friends he says he runs with at night?" Kenzie asked her.

"He mentioned it, but I didn't give it much thought," Brisk said. He can have other friends, mysterious friends. He never elaborated. So who are they and what's so funny?"

Parker made a coyote howl.

"He runs with the coyotes?" Brandy asked.

"Well, the coyotes sometimes track him and howl behind him or parallel him on each side," Kenzie told them with a big smile. "So he says the coyotes are running with him. He loves it. He loves those friends."

"Don't forget his other friend, Kenzie," Zachariah reminded him.

"I'm afraid to ask," Brisk said. "Who?"

"The moon!" Kenzie said, laughing as Parker continued the coyote calls. "He says the moon is a friend you never get tired of. He quietly shows up, gently gets brighter and brighter, and then suddenly disappears."

"He sure is different," Brandy told them.

"Not exactly, Brandy," Kenzie replied. "He's just in tune with nature better than we are. Remember when we ran out here in the moonlight a few weeks ago? Wasn't that awesome? He was trying to share that with us. We need to learn more from him. We experienced the beauty of God's creation hidden at night and Lake opened our eyes to it. We had a great night. We were so blessed by God!"

"We sure were. We have to do it again," Lawrence said.

"It was special night," Brandy added. "It was so beautiful."

"Okay. You can stop howling now, Parker. This is the plan: We have plenty of energy bars, plenty of water, plus, I have a water filter just in case. Team vote. Who wants to head out there?" Everyone's hand went up. "Okay, Parker. Lead on!"

The first hour of the journey was fairly easy on the winding roads. Only a few downed trees and several stream fords were the obstacles. The last two hours became more grueling as they had turned onto an abandoned railroad bed. While the grade was fairly steady, they had to cross Eagle Creek fourteen times. On three of the crossings they were forced to walk across the remaining beams of each bridge, carrying their mountain bikes and balancing themselves at the same time. The rest of the bridges were long ago removed requiring a twenty- to thirty-foot descent down the embankment to the creek and an ascent up the opposite embankment to the railroad bed.

There were two tunnels along the way. The aqueduct tunnel was a quarter of a mile long and filled with about a foot of water. The only light was from each entrance. Each biker stared ahead because the light of the opening at the opposite end was the only guide. Pedaling through the water was painfully slow, but the cool air inside was refreshing. Exiting the tunnel everyone stopped and laughed about going through the dark damp tube. "It's almost like being with Lake. He'd always say 'Biking with Lake isn't just a bike ride, it's an adventure!" Lawrence said.

"He sure got us into some tight scary places," Zachariah said. "But we always ended up later laughing about it! He took us on trips we'd never have attempted. We'd complain along the way, but...we sure had fun!"

Hogback Tunnel was the last obstacle. But as they were closing in, Zachariah yelled, "Stop!" The tunnel was blocked, rocks piled at the entrance.

"Now what do we do?" Brandy asked.

Parker had already begun walking his bike up a four-wheeler trail to the ridgeline. Everyone followed. The climb took half an hour. At the rocky top views could be seen to the north and to the south.

Lawrence looked at Parker and asked with some agitation, "Are you sure we're going in the right direction? This is almost a Lake adventure. One of his crazy trips. Where are we?"

Parker smiled and pointed to a pond on the south side of the ridge. "Yes!" Zachariah exclaimed. "It's on the south side of the ridge. No mountains or hills to block the moonrise or the sunset. Thank you, God!"

They slowly headed down the makeshift trail to the railroad bed at the southern tunnel entrance. A few minutes later, Parker turned right off the railroad bed onto a grass road that went steeply downhill. As the road leveled out, a large meadow came into view. The bikes were left at the tree line, and everyone began walking silently through the wetlands. Songbirds were flying back and forth, singing loudly. Crickets were chanting on both sides of the road. An occasional cicada could be heard from different directions. The fields were full of wildflowers and patches of ripening blueberry bushes.

As they continued on the road, the pond became partially visible to the left but soon disappeared as the road looped in the opposite direction behind a knoll. While they were going up a slight rise in the road, Lawrence stopped them. "Stop, everyone! Listen!" Through the sounds of nature's melody, something different could be heard. "He's here. Listen! He brought his guitar! How weird. How cool!" he said. "Good job, Parker! Thank you, God!"

"What should we do?" Zachariah asked.

"Should we bother him?" Brandy questioned.

"I think he's expecting us, maybe, I hope," Lawrence replied. "He's up there worshipping the Lord on that knoll overlooking the pond all by himself. That's so…beautiful. I think I'm beginning to understand. You know what? I want to join him."

"So do I," Kenzie said. "I want to worship the Lord. Let's go."

When they were at the top of the knoll, the sun was nearing the horizon in the west. The moon was not up yet but the eastern sky was brightening. Lake was softly singing and struggling with the guitar.

When the chorus began, Lake heard the voices of his friends join in, one by one. Although tears filled his eyes, he kept playing, not looking around. He couldn't sing anymore, but the group continued. Parker went up and gently took control of Lake's guitar. Lake stepped back slightly not knowing Lawrence was standing there. Lawrence placed his arm around Lake and whispered, "I'm so sorry, Lake. I'm so sorry." Lake turned his head away and downward but didn't resist the embrace.

After the chorus, Parker played a beautiful musical interlude. Someone began humming along loudly. Tears ran down Lake's cheeks when he recognized it was Kenzie, but he didn't turn around. Then he heard Brisk's recorder join in. Weakened physically from the long overnight run, the bike ride out to Mirror Pond, and the emotional toll, Lake fell to his knees.

Kenzie quickly dropped down next to Lake and placed his arms around him. "Big bro," Kenzie struggled to get out, "I'm glad you're okay. We'll get through this. I know you're very, very tired. Let's stand up," he said as he signaled to Lawrence to help him.

While Lawrence and Kenzie helped Lake stand up, Brisk handed her recorder to Zachariah and wrapped her arms around Lake. She forced his arms around her. "I'm sorry, Lake," she said. "God gave you a full plate, even fuller yesterday and today. I'm with you, Lake. We all are. I know you've only survived by your faith in Christ. It's humans who left you down."

Looking at the ground, Lake addressed the band, "I only wanted you all to excel in all you did, your running, your music, and especially your walk with Jesus. I know I pushed you too hard, too far, too fast. I'm not sorry for that! I just want you to win in your Christian walk. You were my family, my brothers, and my sisters. At least I thought you were until today."

As Parker continued to play, no one said anything. Then Brisk made Lake walk about fifty feet away from the group. Lawrence joined in the music with his guitar and Zachariah with the shakers. Brandy and Kenzie stood together, watching Lake and Brisk. Standing alone, Brisk holding Lake's shoulders tightly with her hands, and their silhouettes against the sunset, she began softly talking to him.

"Lake," she begins, "Kenzie painfully told me about your youth this morning as you instructed him to. He was very reluctant, but he finally told me how your dad beat you kids and mentally abused you, especially you. You always protected, Kenzie."

"That's not what I wanted him to tell you. I don't need to hear it, Brisk," Lake said, tugging to get away and looking intensely at Kenzie.

"You must," she said while her hold on him became stronger. "You must know I understand. I understand why you are still plagued with the night terror attacks. All because your father beat and strangled you one night while you were sleeping and left you for dead, simple because you became a Christian. Kenzie said that's when your school grades plummeted, you went into deep depression, and most painful for you, you lost your musical ability."

"That's not what I wanted him to tell you. Please stop it, Brisk. Please shut up," he pleaded.

Brisk continued, "A year later, in deep depression over the night terrors, still too young to understand what happened, you turned to your pastor for help. Then one night, when church was open for all-night prayer, you walked miles just to be there. You just wanted to pray. Your pastor saw how vulnerable you were, and while you were praying, he called two of his friends. Leaving the church to head home, you were kidnapped. How evil that was! How terrible! You never told anyone what happened except the police. Then in court, this pastor testified that you were a streetwalker. You, in your innocence, thought it made sense since you were a paperboy. But later in life, you realize what he really was saying. He was only protecting his friends. When your life was opened up in that courtroom, you endured it all alone. Then they were set free. You were beaten again by your father. What you believed your father did to your mother in her sleep, the same thing he did to you. It took you a few years to piece it all together. He also told me how you protected him the other week when your father beat him up pretty bad. I'll never forget that precious boy's bloody face when you brought him to the Eddy. You even took a few punches for him and, grabbing your father's fists, told your father never to hit anyone again. You could have nailed him, but you didn't because of your biblical respect for parents.

"Now I understand why you are so quiet, so sensitive, so needing to be alone. If you can forgive me and give me a second chance, I'll respect those boundaries and be sensitive to your pain. What Kenzie and I don't understand is what happened at North Mountain yesterday. Are you able to tell me now? I just want to understand it all, Lake."

"I'm sorry that happened that day, but it was him," Lake said, trying not to look at Brisk.

"Who?" Brisk asked.

"He was that pastor. It brought back all those memories. I wanted to kill him. I hate him! He should die!" Busting away from Brisk, he screamed at her, "I hate me! I hate me! I hate me! That's not what I wanted Kenzie to tell you! I should have never had Kenzie say anything to you. I only wanted him to tell you my thoughts toward you. I hate me! Go away and leave me alone! You can't possibly like me, no one can! Don't you understand that! Just go far, far away! Forever!"

Lawrence yelled at Lake, "Don't talk to my sister that way!"

"Don't tell me what to do," he yelled back and then bolted in Lawrence's direction, but Kenzie and Zachariah rushed in and stopped him. Lake turned and began to walk away. Kenzie ran over and grabbed his arm. They struggled, but Kenzie wrestled Lake to the ground. "Stop it, Lake, stop it now! This is not the strong brother I know. Calm down, big bro. Just chill out," he said.

"Calm down? That's not what I wanted you to tell her. You always want to publish our family's dirty laundry. Well, you succeeded in destroying my life so just get married and move away. Let me up."

"You're not going anywhere until you calm down."

Lake responded, "You got me only because I'm so tired. I could kick your ass."

"You could," Kenzie said with a smile, "but you won't."

"Kenzie, you have it all, looks, brains, personality, all these friends of yours. Why don't you take yourself and all your friends home and leave me alone."

"These are your friends too."

"Have any of these 'friends' punched you or slapped you?"

"Lake, these are your friends. They are here because they love you. I love you. I will not leave you here alone. You're the bestest brother in the world. You are my best friend. You the only family I have now. What's your favorite verse?"

"What?" Lake asked surprised.

"Tell me. Tell us. Tell your soul, tell your flesh, tell your spirit. What's your favorite scripture? Recite it out loud for us to hear. Do what you tell us to do. Fight the enemy. Come on, stubborn boy."

"I'm not stubborn."

"Yes, you are. You are the king of stubborn."

"Name one time."

"Let's see. How about the time Dad told you he was coming to that race in Front Royal to watch you. I told you he wouldn't show. You got mad at me and said you'd sit there until midnight and wait. Well, he didn't show. He was home laughing about it. I came down at 11:00 p.m., and you were sitting their shivering under a streetlight all by yourself waiting. That's stubborn. Then you made me wait until midnight before we went home. That's super stubborn."

"I wasn't being stubborn. I really believed he'd show up. I just believed. I just stupidly believed! I was stupid. Thank you for reminding me of that special family moment."

"I'm sorry, Lake. I shouldn't have brought that up. Now, I'll ask you one more time. What is your favorite verse?"

"Just get off me and leave me alone before I get really mad."

"What is your favorite verse?"

Parker, still playing the guitar and listening to the conversation, strummed hard across all the guitar strings, grabbing everyone's attention. He walked over to the group and looked at Lake on the ground, then looked up at the sky and, with great difficulty, recited Lake's favorite scripture: "You reign...forever! You have...established... Your throne...for judgment! You will...judge the world...

in right...eous...ness! You will gov...ern us...with justice! You are a refuge...for the oppressed, a stronghold...in time...of trouble!"

"Parker, don't, it's too hard for you," Lake pleaded.

"Those who...know your name...will trust in you, for... You, Lord, have...never...for...saken those who...seek you!" Then Parker reached down to Lake. Lake hesitated briefly then took Parker's hand and, with some help from Kenzie, stood up.

Lake suddenly grabbed Kenzie and raised his fist. "That's not what I wanted you to tell her, you little..." but he didn't finish what he was about to say.

"Little what, Lake. Punk?" Kenzie said calmly. "What's that fist for? You know you would never call me that and you would never hit me. You know why? Because you are free from it all. You are not like our father. You are a new creature. The curse is broken, you have been set free."

Lake pushed Kenzie away and began walking toward the sunset. Then he turned around. "Kenzie," he said, "why don't you and your friends just go home. I don't need anyone. I never did. Just get out of here and leave me alone." He turned and continued to walk away.

"Tell me you honestly believe what you are saying is true?" Kenzie yelled.

Lake stopped. After a long pause, he turned and said, "I really don't know. I just, I just feel so bad inside. I really do hate me. So much has happened yesterday and today and so much pain is brought back to life. I hid it so well for so long. I wish, sometimes I wish I was never born."

"Well, I am glad you were, and I like you just the way you are, wild and weird," Kenzie said with a laugh, trying to get Lake to smile.

"I'm not amused, Kenzie. I'm sorry."

After a few minutes of quiet awkwardness, Lawrence broke the silence. "Lake, Satan was trying to drive our team apart. We all stumbled, especially me. But like you said, we got to get up and continue running. Lake, I'm so sorry. Marilyn and I were engaged two years ago and then she went out with some other guy. When I thought you cheated on my sister, especially with Marilyn, my anger got the best of me, and I lost it. I feel terrible, Lake, really, really terrible."

"Looks like it's going to be another beautiful night," Lake said while scanning the sky.

"You are so slick about changing the subject, especially when it's something you don't want to talk about!" Lawrence told him. "Listen to me, Lake. I am eternally grateful for you leading Marilyn to the Lord. Maybe she and I can get back together again. But you're our spiritual leader, and for now, the question is how are you going to get us out of here?"

"Now that you need help getting out of here, I'm your friend again?'"

"You never stopped being my friend," Lawrence told him.

"Compassion. Why do I have the gift of compassion? It'll get you guys out of here, but it doesn't get me anywhere," Lake grudgingly replied.

"That's a wonderful gift. Caring for other people," Brisk told him.

"Wonderful if you're on the receiving end. Okay, okay, I'll help you get out of here. I guess I'm good for something." He took a deep breath and was visibly showing his fatigue. "It's getting dark. We better…head out. It's a two-hour ride. Do any of you have your headlamps?"

"Yes, you always told us be prepared," Lawrence replied. "Hey, it took us about forty minutes to get to the knoll we usually go to, then, maybe three hours or so to get here. How could it be a two-hour ride?"

"You must have come the long way. I came over Keating Road, that new forestry road before the knoll," Lake said. "It's not on the current map."

"You did know we were coming, didn't you?" Zachariah said with a cautious laugh.

"No. I didn't even think about it," Lake replied. "If I wanted you to find me, I would have parked my Jeep at the gate to Keating Road. I figured if anyone would look for me, they go to the knoll because I parked there. I know how to cover my tracks. But you were all pretty smart and figured it out. After all that happened today, why would I expect you? I just wanted my time alone with the Lord. I felt so many emotions today. I guess I was just trying to keep myself together."

"Let's go sing one more time then get out of Dodge. Um, maybe in a few days, we can have a time of healing at the Eddy. I mean, if you want to," Lawrence suggested.

"You all can sing. I don't feel like it. I think I'll close and sell the Eddy and move back to Dawson City."

"Don't talk like that, you're just tired. Come on, let's go sing," Brisk told him, gently coaxing him to join the rest of the group.

As they sang and prayed, Lake remained quiet. After retrieving their instruments and their bikes, they returned to the knoll and watched the last colors of the sunset and the moonrise, praising God for his creativity.

"Last night was full moon and already you can see it beginning to fade. But God will restore it in a few weeks," Lake said softly.

"He can restore and makes all things new. He's the stronghold in times of trouble. He's the father...of the...fatherless," Brisk said softly while looking directly at Lake.

"It's starting to get dark, let's go," Lake said as he changed the subject. "Once we make it out to Keating Road, we may be able to ride without the headlamps because of the moonlight." He quietly turned and began biking. A line of six mountain bikes, one by one, joined him. Stopping at the tree line, Lake turned to look back toward the pond. "Look, did you see that?" he asked the others.

"No, what?" Zachariah asked.

"Just watch out across the pond," Lake told him.

Several miles away, lighting bolts flashed, illuminating a distance cloud and reflecting its yellow and orange colors across the still waters of the pond.

"Wow!" Lawrence exclaimed. "I've never seen anything like that before. Where's the thunder?"

"It's too far away to be heard," Lake replied.

"That is absolutely beautiful," Brisk added. "It's like the pond is a mirror."

"No wonder they call it Mirror Pond," Zachariah added.

"God never stops showing us his glory and his creativity. It's all around us. The sunset, the moonrise, the lightning…listen, a whip-poor-will. All we have to do is look and listen. Nature testifies to God's existence," Lake told them. "Let's head out."

Lawrence yelled, "Ready?"

"Ready!" they responded. They all shouted together, "Blessed be your name today, Lord God!" except for Lake.

Lake said, "Let's go," and began biking. The rest looked at each other.

Kenzie said, "He'll be okay. Give him time." The seven mountain bikers disappeared into the woods.

9

All out of Love

The funeral service for Mr. Nidhatak was at the church on Tuesday morning. Lake, Brisk, Kenzie, and Brandy arrived in Lake's Jeep. Just as they were getting out Mrs. Bentley, the pastor's wife, rushed up to them. "Good morning, everyone. Lakeland and Mackenzie, Pastor Bentley needs to see you two alone right away. He's with some other people in there now, so please have a seat outside his office until he's calls you. I'll walk Brisk and Brandy in."

"What's it about, Mrs. Bentley?" Lake asked.

"Hurry in, boys. The service starts in ten minutes," she said.

"I'll be in shortly, Brisk," Lake said as he hugged her. Kenzie hugged Brandy and winked at her then said, "I'll be right back."

"Wonder what he wants," Lake asked as he and Kenzie headed for the office.

"Probably last-minute details. You look good dressed up. You should do it more often," Kenzie said, complimenting Lake.

"No, I don't, and no, I won't. I hate it. Let's get this day over with," Lake responded. "Kenzie, do you think God really loves me?"

"That's a dumb question. Of course he does."

"Sometimes, I just don't know. I just wonder, I mean, so much junk has happened, maybe he doesn't like me."

"Lake, you think no one likes you. You know God loves you, don't you?"

"The Bible says he does."

"Said and done."

Pastor Bentley's office door was closed so Lake and Kenzie sat on the chairs in the hallway as Mrs. Bentley instructed them. After a few minutes, Kenzie stood up and began peeking in the door's window. "What are you doing?" Lake asked.

"Just scanning the territory," Kenzie said. "It's something my brother taught me."

"You're snooping, I don't snoop," Lake told him.

"Call it whatever you want, scanning the territory, snooping. Lake!" Kenzie half-shouted. "There is a dude in there. He looks exactly like you!"

"Kenzie, don't make fun of people."

"Wow! There is this beautiful girl too. She is beautiful! I wish I could meet her!" Kenzie told Lake.

"Kenzie, you're engaged. Your life is almost over."

Kenzie grabbed Lake and pulled him to the door. "Look, you bozo!"

"Ah! You're right! He does look like me. He could be a twin. Wonder who he is. Sit down! Here comes Bentley!

Pastor Bentley opened the door. "Good morning, Lake, Kenzie. Please come in." Lake and Kenzie walked in and stood in front of Pastor Bentley's desk. The young man and women who had been talking to Pastor Bentley stood up facing Lake and Kenzie. Pastor Bentley said, "This Lakeland Nidhatak and his brother Mackenzie Nidhatak. Lake and Kenzie, please meet Llewellyn and Lydia." They all shook hands.

Kenzie said, "Pleased to meet you, is this your wife?"

"Nice to meet you. No, this is my sister," Llewellyn responded. When he said that, Kenzie poked Lake's side with his elbow.

"You certainly look familiar, Llewellyn," Lake said.

"Well, there is a reason for that," Pastor Bentley told him. "Please, everyone be seated." Pastor Bentley sat down and looked around, searching for the proper words to say. "Lake, Kenzie, your father was not a very faithful man to your mother."

"We're very aware of that. Where are you going with this and why now?" Lake asked.

"Boys," Pastor Bentley started.

"We're not boys, we're grown men. Now get to the point, I have a funeral to attend," Lake told him with some agitation.

Then Kenzie stood up. "You're going to tell us this is our brother and our sister, aren't you?"

"Yes, Kenzie, this is your brother and your sister," Pastor Bentley affirmed to him.

"Please excuse me," a polite and tearful Kenzie said to everyone. "Brandy is waiting for me. Nice to meet you all, I think." He turned and left the room.

"Lake, I just found out about this an hour ago. They found out last night about your father and drove all night to be here. There was no easy way to convey this to you and no good time, I'm sorry," Pastor Bentley told him.

"Well, I guess we better be going up to the funeral," Lake said as he stood up. "Where is your mother?" he suddenly asked.

"She is at home," Lydia told him. "She hasn't seen our father for nearly twenty years and felt it wasn't appropriate to be here. Llewellyn and I wanted to come. We just felt we needed to."

"How old are you?"

"I'm twenty-one, and Llewellyn is twenty-three," Lydia answered.

"When we lived in Dawson City, my dad would come down to the states almost every year to stock up on supplies. That would be about in that time frame. My mom watched three little boys in the Yukon wilderness while he was here sowing his wild oats. Where are you staying?" Lake asked.

"We haven't had time to look for a motel. We'll wait until after the service," Llewellyn said.

"You will be staying at the Eddy. We have a lot to discuss," Lake told them. He drew a map on a piece of paper. "Here are the directions and mileage to the Eddy and my cabin. I call it Base Camp, you'll see the sign. It is unlocked. I probably won't be there until late so just make yourselves at home. Please understand if Kenzie or I aren't at our best today. It's been difficult."

"We understand. We'll keep a low profile at the services. My sister and I thank you for your hospitality," Llewellyn told him as he shook Lake's hand.

Lake left the office and headed down the hall alone. He heard weeping in one of the Sunday schoolrooms, so he stopped and looked it. There was Kenzie leaning against a blackboard, crying. "Kenzie," Lake whispered as he walked in.

When Kenzie heard Lake, he turned to face him and said, "You knew all along, didn't you? Didn't you?"

"Kenzie," Lake started.

"Don't Kenzie me. I'm your brother. Can't you tell me this stuff? Couldn't you have warned me this might happen? You are so weird, just like everyone says. I'm sorry. I don't mean that, I just don't understand you." Then Kenzie walked around Lake and left the room.

Lake walked over to the blackboard and touched the wet spot left from Kenzie's tears. "I was only trying to protect you, little bro."

Kenzie walked into the sanctuary and sat down by Brisk and Brandy. Brandy asked, "What did Pastor Bentley want to talk to you and Lake about?"

"How's your car running?" Kenzie snapped. Brisk's and Brandy's eyes got large, and they sat back in their seats, knowing not to ask any further questions. Lake came in and quietly sat down, not saying a word. Pastor Bentley came in with Llewellyn and Lydia, seating them on the other side of the room. He went to the front and began the service, which was short as Lake and Kenzie had requested. After everyone paid their respects to Mr. Nidhatak, the funeral procession was organized, and they proceeded to the cemetery.

At the cemetery, the pallbearers removed Mr. Nidhatak's casket from the hearse. In front were Lake and Mackenzie, then Zachariah, Parker, Lawrence, and Llewellyn. Pastor Bentley spoke for a few minutes and then prayed. After the service, Lake stood nearby alone, looking toward the mountains. Kenzie walked over and said, "Lake, it's time to go."

"I was only trying to protect you. I really didn't know for sure. I only heard the rumors," Lake said to Kenzie's while keeping his eyes on the mountains. "They'll be staying at the Eddy. I felt compassion on them, and I thought we all need to talk." Kenzie and Lake walked to the limo where the other pallbearers were standing waiting for him. Brisk and Brandy gave Lake and Kenzie a kiss and a hug. Lake got in not saying a word to the girls.

Brisk whispered to Kenzie, "Is he going to be all right? His mood has changed even from this morning."

As Kenzie walked Brisk and Brandy to their limo, he replied, "You promised to respect his boundaries, so when he takes off this afternoon, let him be."

"You think he's going to run away again?" Brisk asked.

"He's didn't run away before and he's not running away now, he's finding his solitude. He sat through the viewing, the funeral, and next the dinner. I know my brother and he's ready to burst."

"But do you think he'll be all right?" Brisk asked again.

"I hope so, but there is little I can do about it. The only thing I'm worried about is he was questioning me if I thought God could love him," Kenzie replied.

"What did you tell him?" Brandy asked.

"I said of course he does. But we do view God as we view our earthly father, so can you imagine what thoughts have been going through his head."

"Who is the other pallbearer?" Brisk asked. "He looks like Lake. He could be your brother."

"He is. Surprise!" Kenzie said with a sigh.

"What?" a startled Brisk asked.

"And that beautiful redhead, she's our sister. Surprise again! Let's not talk about that today, or tomorrow, or ever. I need no more surprises."

The front limo beeped its horn. "Gotta go. Lake can explain someday," Kenzie said. "I'll see you when we get back to the church. I love you, Brisk. I love you, Brandy." He gave each a hug and then ran to his limo.

At the church dining hall, as they were eating, a man came up to Lake and Kenzie and said, "I'm sorry about your father, Lake and Kenzie. He was thought of highly in the community. He was a wonderful father to you and a wonderful husband to your mother. You have my sympathy."

Lake dropped his fork and stared at the man. Kenzie looked at Lake then to the man and said, "Ah, thank you, sir. Ah, we appreciate everyone's sympathy."

Kenzie looked at Lake and said, "Lake, just stay calm. I'm staying calm, even after the bombshell this morning that you forgot to tell me about. So for another hour or so, we'll just stay calm and then all this will be over. Okay?"

"I must be at the wrong freaking funeral. All these strangers suddenly pop up out of nowhere and tell me how saintly he was. I just want to punch them all as hard as I possibly can. This is a bunch of bullshit. I'm leaving before I puke my guts out."

"Lake, please don't leave, not now, I need you," Kenzie pleaded.

Standing up and looking at Brandy, Lake said, "Kenzie, you don't need me anymore."

Lake turned and walked away then he turned around and came back to Brisk. "I'll see you at the Eddy tonight, Brisk. I'm sorry, I have to leave." Lake turned and walked away. Several people spoke to him as he walked to the door but he ignored them.

"You were right, Kenzie, he was going to take off," Brisk said. "I want to follow him, but you said to respect his boundaries. It tears me apart inside to just sit here and do nothing."

Suddenly, Lake came back into the church dining hall and walked over to Brisk. He reached out his hand to her. She looked at Kenzie and Brandy then back to Lake. She stood up, and he grabbed her hand, turned, and with Brisk in tow left the church.

Brandy looked at Kenzie, who shrugged his shoulders and said, "I can't figure him out, so don't even ask."

10

Broken

Lake escorted Brisk to his Jeep, helping her in and even buckling her seatbelt. Lake walked around the Jeep and got in. He started the Jeep and looked up at the mountains. Brisk reached over with her hand gently sliding it across his face to his neck and then massaged his neck. He placed his head down and momentarily begins to cry but caught himself. He took a deep breath to gain his self-control.

"Lake, I'll follow you on whatever adventure you have for us today."

Lake took her hand and kissed it then began to drive away. After a silent hour on the highway, he turned up a rough forestry road. The steep climb required four-wheel drive. After bouncing for half an hour, the road ended at a large open area of barren smooth rock with a view. Lake got out and walked to Brisk's side of the Jeep and helped her out. They stood together and took in the view of the mountains and the river below.

"Lake, this is so beautiful. How do you find all these wonderful places?" she asked.

"I don't waste my time watching television, I explore God's creativity. This place reminds me of the Dome up at Dawson City in the Yukon. I remember every now and then I'd hike up or Dad would drive us up. It was always windy up there, but I didn't care because I could see forever. I could see Dawson City down below. I could see the awesome Yukon River as it was heading to Alaska and on to the Bering Strait. Sometimes the Midnight Sun. Sometimes the Northern Lights. It was such a happy time. We were a happy family. When I come here, I imagine I'm still there and how things could have been. Every spring when the geese fly north, I cry."

"Why do you cry when you see the geese?" Brisk softly asked him.

"I want to fly north with them. I want to know how things could have been. I want a happy family. Oh, if I could fly with them," he replied as he pulled Brisk close and hugged her from the back. "Brisk, my soul is so torn inside. It hurts so bad. Everything I suppressed for so long has come alive again."

"Lake, God loves you so much, I know you know that, don't you?" Brisk asked Lake but got no reply. She turned around and faced him. "You know that, don't you?"

"The Bible says he does, but I'm not sure what love is. Even if I did know, I can honestly say I'm all out of love. Why do I miss Sheba so bad and not feel any loss today for my dad, the only emotion I have for him is anger," Lake responded. "Sheba was the only flesh I knew that loved me, and I knew I loved her. I miss her so bad. It hurts so bad, Brisk." She held him tight and whispered, "It's all right to cry. Let it go, Lake."

"Big boys don't cry," he told her. "Big boys don't cry."

After a few quiet minutes, Lake said, "Brisk, will you sit here on this rock while I pray to God? I'm usually alone, but I need to do this now." He held her hand as she sat down. He walked back to the Jeep to retrieve his Bible then gave it to Brisk. Then he walked twenty feet from her and looked out over the valley. A slight breeze was blowing his tie around. He knelt and looked to the sky. "Father God. Show me your love. I need it so much right now. I know what your Word says, but I need you to show me. I'm not testing you, I just need that touch please. I'm so empty, so broken. I'm just a wasteland."

As Lake knelt in silence, Brisk walked up behind him and read, "I remember my affliction and my wondering, the bitterness, and the gall. I well remember them, and my soul is downcast within me. Yet this I call to mind and have hope: Because of the Lord's great love, because of the Lord's great love, we are not consumed, for his compassions never fail. They are new like the dew every morning that we live: Father great is your faithfulness. I say to myself 'The lord is my portion therefore I will wait for him."

Lake sat on the ground and buried his head between his knees. Brisk laid her hand on his back and prayed silently, holding her right hand up to the Lord. Lake stood up and walked over to the cliff. Looking to the sky, he screamed, "I don't understand you! I don't understand you! What do you want from me? You win, oh, Father God! I'm broken, I'm so broken. Again! Just take me home. I don't want to play this game of life anymore. I can bear it no more!"

Lake walked back to Brisk. He had tears in his eyes. "Let's go for a ride, Brisk." They got in the Jeep and headed back down the mountain. Lake drove for an hour then came to a small town.

"This is a beautiful little town. Where are we at?" Brisk asked.

"Round Island," Lake told her. "This is where my grandfather was born." Suddenly they came upon some backed-up traffic. "What's this about?" he asked Brisk.

"Looks like a carnival," Brisk replied. "Look, there's a banner across the road. Says 'Borough of Round Island Bicentennial Celebration.' Parade at 2:00 p.m. Then a block party at 3:00 p.m."

"Looks like a 15K race at 6:00 p.m."

"What time is it now?" Lake asked.

"It's five forty-seven. Why?" she asked.

Lake looked around in all directions. Then he did a U-turn and pulled into the first parking spot he could find. "I got to run this race, Brisk. I really believe God wants me to."

"Okay, Lake, I'll cheer you on, but one question: how are you going to run in those clothes?" she asked.

"A true runner is always prepared." He stood beside his jeep and took off his shirt, revealing a tank top. Then he slid off his pants showing his runner shorts. He tossed them as well as the socks and dress shoes in the back of the Jeep. Then he opened a daypack and pulled out his running shoes and socks and put them on.

"You are so funny," Brisk said as she watched him.

"Come with me to register, okay?" he asked her.

"Of course!" she said.

They walked down the main street of the little town and found the starting point for the race. Lake registered and received his number. "Look, I'm number 57. Cool T-shirt too. Here are the Jeep keys, the race packet with all the freebees, and the T-shirt. Let's take them back to the Jeep."

"I don't think we have time, Lake. They are lining up now for the start," Brisk told Lake.

Someone yelled, "Ready, set," then a gun when off and the runners started.

"Lake, you're missing the start. Run!" Brisk said, laughing.

Lake looked at her and said, "Thank you for being here with me," and then he hugged and kissed her. "Gotta run!" he said as he turned and began chasing the running crowd. At a distance, he turned and waved at her. She blew him a kiss, and while running backward, he pretended he caught it. Then he turned and began accelerating toward the runners.

Lake ran down the main street of the little town trying to catch the running pack. People watching the race thought all the runners had past so they began walking in the street. Lake had to maneuver around them for several blocks, saying, "Excuse me, pardon me, coming through."

At the two-mile mark, he caught the end runners. Suddenly, a steep hill came into sight. Many people were walking but Lake easily continued and passed many. The road leveled out with a long straightaway revealing a long line of runners. The front runners could be seen far in the distance. Lake kept pressing on, continually passing. He watched the scenery around him and began praising God for the beautiful fields and mountains. "A beautiful day," he'd remark to others but got little response.

At a water stop a volunteer fireman told Lake, "You're number 10. There's a big hill ahead, so drink plenty of water."

"Thank you, sir," Lake responded. "Thank you for the info and for being out here for us today." He began running and continued to catch runners. Another steep hill came into view. More runners were walking. "Ninth, eighth, seventh, sixth," he counted to himself as he passed them. Halfway up the hill, two runners were sitting on the guardrails, sweating profusely. "Hey, guys, need a drink or something?" Lake asked. "I have some power gels if you need them."

"No, but thanks," one said. "Just not used to the mountains and the heat."

"What mountain? You mean this hill?" Lake asked seriously.

The two runners began to laugh. "Three runners ahead of you," one said. The other added, "The way you're going up this mountain you should be able to catch them."

"I just run for fun. I never win. Come on, guys, we're almost to the top then its four miles downhill. Come on," Lake told them while running backward. "The hard part is nearly over."

"Good luck," they each said, making no attempt to get off the guardrails. Lake turned around and continued up the hill. "Now I'm in fourth place. This can't be right." Rounding a corner, he passed two more runners.

"Good run," one said.

"You'll catch me on the downhill, I'm sure," Lake told him. "Come on and stay with me. We're almost to the top," but they just signaled him to go on. A short time later Lake crested the mountain. A brush truck with its emergency lights flashing along with its crew of volunteer firemen was waiting to hand the runners water. "Congratulations, you're in first place," the vehicle's driver said. "When you hit the highway just ahead, make a right and its four miles downhill. Take it in."

"I should be in second place. Where is the other runner?" Lake asked. Some of the firemen pointed over the guardrails where a runner was bent over, vomiting. "Oh, well, thanks for all your help. Hope he's better. He'll probably catch me."

Lake continued to the highway, crossing four lanes and began heading downhill. Several state police cruisers were positioned along the intersection to help with the traffic. One cruiser pulled out and crossed the road onto the berm in front of Lake. He turned on the emergency lights and began leading Lake the four miles down the mountain. "This can be for real," Lake said out loud. "Where is everyone?"

He began to run harder. The cruiser stayed fifty feet ahead, keeping pace with him. People were beeping, waving, and cheering Lake on as they drove by. One mile from the finish Lake turned around one last time seeing no one. *This can't be for real*, he thought to himself. Then he almost stopped when he realized what was actually happening. His eyes began to swell with tears, and he spoke out loud, "My God, my God, you are showing me your love. This is all because of you. Oh, precious Lord, you do love me. You do love me. You love me! Thank you, thank you. I give it all back to you. All glory is yours! All glory is yours! Thank you. You do love me!"

The cruiser led a smiling Lake back through town and to the finish line. People were cheering him along and cameras flashed as he crossed the finish line. Lake stopped running and walked to cool down. He pointed to the sky and yelled, "You are an awesome God. Please help the others finish their race today. Blessed is your name!"

Brisk ran to Lake. They hugged and spun in a circle. "You came in first, Lake! I'm so proud of you!" she said.

"It was God! He was showing me he loved me. He controlled the events just to prove he loved me. It was against the odds. He is an awesome God. He loves me, Brisk! He loves me! My God really loves me!"

"Of course he does! He loves Lakeland Nidhatak," Brisk said as she hugged him.

Lake and Brisk remained at the finish line and applauded as each runner crossed. When the last runner came in, Lake walked over and congratulated him. "Great run," Lake said. "What's your name?"

"Benjamin. I came in last. Pretty bad. What place did you come in?" the out-of-breath runner asked him.

"It's not about where you placed, it's about finishing. You did more today than 99 percent of the people in this country. What a hard course! You finished. We finished! Congratulation!" Lake told him.

"Thanks, guy. It was a tough course. Maybe, maybe I'll do better next year," he said.

"That's the spirit! Have an incentive, have a vision, then make it happen! Congratulations again!"

A short time later, the race officials called the names of the first, second and third place runners. Each was given their respective trophy and several group pictures were taken. After the last camera flash, Lake held his trophy to the sky and said, "This belongs to you. Thank you!"

Lake spoke with a few runners and thanked the race officials. Just as Brisk and Lake were about to leave, Benjamin walked up to them. "You came in first and you congratulated me? Why?" he asked.

"Because you finished, you didn't give up. It's not about what place you came in, it's about persevering and finishing the race you started. You finished. I think that's so great," Lake told him. "Did you set a goal of doing this race next year and moving up in the ranks?"

"That's my goal, you convinced me to do that. Thank you," Benjamin replied.

"Do you have a pen, Brisk?" Lake asked.

"Yes, here, Lake," she responded.

Lake wrote his name and number on the bottom of the trophy. "Here, I loan this to you for a year as a reminder of your vision for next year. I wrote my name and number on the bottom if you need a coach."

"You're in for adventure if you call him," Brisk said with a smile.

"Wow, thanks, ah, Lake. I'll give you a call," Benjamin said as he read the name on the bottom of the trophy. "I have to go, thanks again, Lake, and what is your name?" he asked Brisk.

"I'm sorry," Lake said. "Benjamin, this is Brisk. Brisk, this is Benjamin."

"Pleased to me you. Got to go, thanks again," Benjamin told them.

"Blessings to you," Lake told him.

"Blessings?" Benjamin asked.

"We'll discuss that next time," Lake said as he waved and began walking in the other direction with Brisk. "I love divine appointments, don't you?" he said to Brisk who nodded in agreement. Lake stopped and closed his eyes for a few seconds. "Are you okay?" Brisk asked.

"Yeah, just a little light-headed and a killer headache. It sure was hot climbing that mountain."

"Did you drink anything on the racecourse?"

"No. It was so unbelievable what was happening I don't think I even considered it."

"Let's go get some ice cream," Brisk suggested.

"That sounds great," Lake answered as they walked hand in hand down the street. "What a race. I never, never would have thought that I'd be led four miles by a police car to the finish line. It was four whole miles! It was so awesome. God was showing me he loved me. It was all planned by him."

"He always loved you," Brisk replied. "But you needed him to display his love to you. You always said his love is all around, in the mountains, in the trees, in the stars. You always are pointing out his creativity and love, why didn't you believe it for yourself?"

"I did believe it, but I really needed to hear it really loud. And he made it loud and clear today."

As they walked in front of a small-town park, full of flowering ornamental trees and shrubs, Lake saw a bench and said, "I have to sit down, sorry."

After they sat down, Brisk looked at Lake and asked, "How loud do I need to be until you believe me?"

"During the last few days, you made it loud and clear to me. I wouldn't have come back for you at church if I didn't think you did," he told her.

"If I did what?" Brisk asked.

"If, if, if you really…if you really, ah, liked me," Lake said shyly then hugged her and gave her a long kiss. "Let's get some ice cream and head home. I see a stand up on the next corner."

After getting their ice cream, Lake and Brisk slowly strolled back to where the Jeep was parked. "What a day, Brisk, from despair to blessings. I know there is still a lot that I will have to deal with, but realizing God and you are beside me, I mean, he'll fix everything, won't he?"

"He'll only give you what you can handle," Brisk told him. "You were at your breaking point, Lake. Maybe that's what needed to happen."

"Is this the right way to the Jeep. I forget where we parked. Anyway, what's he want with me? I always wanted to do whatever he wanted me to do. I just felt he didn't want me. What do you think?"

"I can see the Jeep from here. As for what does God want, I think, for now, you just need to rest in him. You just need to rest, period, Lake. You've hardly slept in four days. You even look beat. Your forehead is hot, are you going to be all right?"

"Yeah, I'm feeling it, but I'm fine. I always thought I ran well when I was tired, and today proved it."

As they were nearing Lake's Jeep, he said excitedly, "Listen! Hear that?"

"That's a beautiful songbird, what is it, Lake?"

"Well, when I through-hiked the Appalachian Trail, I always heard it and called it the Home Bird because it reminded me of home. Now, at home, I always call it the Trail Bird because it reminds me of the trail."

"What kind of bird is it, Lake?" she asked.

"It's a wood thrush. Listen, its sounds like a flute. Isn't it beautiful! I love running in the woods and hearing it just before dark. It's a sound I long for to begin in the spring. It's one item on my list of things I must hear or see to know its spring."

"What are the other things on your list?"

"Oh, see a robin, see colt's feet, hear spring peepers, and of course, see and hear the geese heading north."

Just then they arrived at the Jeep. As Lake opened the door for Brisk, he said, "Look up the river! Isn't that beautiful?" he exclaimed as he pointed to the west. "Another beautiful sunset!"

"Yes, it is beautiful," she said. "You always said no sunset is ever the same. God's creativity never stops."

"Hear that in the trees? Katydids! They start their noise about this time, the end of July. I love to listen to them at night. Crickets on the ground, katydids in the trees, I love a full moon night and to be out in the woods listening to them. Maybe we can get the gang together and do that for the August full moon! Another overnight run!"

"You are so funny. You know and love nature like no one else I know. And you realize it is God's creativity. I think we could do another midnight run. They'd love it."

"A difficult day has ended with so many blessings. It turned into a perfect evening. The crickets, the katydids, the trail bird, and you! All my friends are here!" Lake said with a big smile.

"Lake, you have other friends."

"No comment at this time," he replied.

"Lake!"

"Brisk!" he said with a smile.

Just then, Trooper Allen stepped out of an unmarked patrol car behind Lake's Jeep. "Good evening, Brisk, Lakeland."

"Ah, hi, John, I mean Trooper Allen, what are you doing here, this is a different county?"

"Lakeland, this is Trooper Bauer and I afraid we're looking for you."

"Why?" Lake asked visibly getting upset.

"Lake, an arrest warrant has been issued for you concerning your attack on Pastor Avalon."

"I didn't attack him. I defended myself from his lies."

"Lakeland, step here. I need to take you to District Justice office in Mountain Springs."

"For what?" Lake asked.

Trooper Bauer began reading the charges: "Assault and battery, terroristic threats, trespassing, breaking and entering—"

"That's baloney!" Lake interrupted.

"Lakeland, let's go," John demanded.

"No! I'm not going anywhere. Don't ruin this night...please. Don't ruin it."

"Lake, John is your friend, relax," Brisk pleaded with him. "John, he hasn't slept in days and today was his father funeral. Can't this wait, please?"

"I'm sorry I have no choice, Brisk. Lakeland, step over here," he said as he pulled out handcuffs.

"Lake, just go with him he's your friend."

Lake began walking backward while staring at the handcuffs. "I thought he was my friend…but I was wrong. He's a friend of Avalon. He's tossing our friendship out for Avalon because Avalon is a big ass of a preacher. That's all. He hates me too."

"John, he's tired and talking nonsense," Brisk said. Then turning to Lake, she said, "Lake, stop it now, please. I'll follow you to Mountain Springs, okay?"

Lake began breathing heavily and looked confused. "You said God only gives you what you can handle, apparently he wasn't finished yet!" He suddenly turned around and started running away, but two Round Island police officers were watching the situation just in case Trooper Allen needed any assistance. They tackled and handcuffed Lake, and because he refused to walk, he was dragged back to police cruiser. After Trooper Bauer read him his rights, Lake was placed in the back seat.

"Thank you, guys, for your assistance. I figured this would happen. I'm glad I radioed you."

"You're more than welcome. We don't want this trash on our streets."

"He's not trash, he's my son. He just lost his temper one day in church, that's all. Usually a good kid."

"Oh, sorry, we didn't know."

"No need to be sorry, I understand where you are coming from. There are bad people out there, but this one just needs a little help understanding life. I'm afraid he's learning it the hard way. Good night."

"Good night."

"Brisk, I'm sorry you had to be here. I'm sorry this all had to happen."

"Can I speak to him for a second, John, please?" John didn't say anything but opened the back door for Brisk. "Lake," she said gently, "remember all that happened today, God loves you. Everything happens for a reason to those that believe. You know he loves you, right?"

Lake, lying on the backseat, turned his head slowly toward her and said, "I don't know what to think. It's always something. One step forward, ten steps back. I just want to go home. I just want to go home. I want to go home, please." Then he looked at John. "What are you all looking at? You don't give a…"

John closed the door and began to walk Brisk to Lake's Jeep. "Trooper Bauer was sent down here, and I got permission to assist him, being I knew Lake. I'll call Mackenzie and ask him to meet us at the District Justice and hopefully he can post bail."

"You called him your son, why?"

"Well, because I consider him just that, my son, I always have. Both him and Mackenzie. I have three beautiful daughters, but no biological son. So I always thought of them as my sons. I've known Lakeland since he was about eleven years old. Helped him out now and then. Now with his father gone, in time, maybe I can say that openly and proudly."

"I think he'd like to know that, John. Someday, maybe you need to tell him."

"He'll be mad at me for a few days, but maybe I will."

"When we all were at the Eddy, the night Kenzie proposed to Brandy, I waited until everyone left and talked with Lake. I asked about you and he said he wished you were his father. He said you were tough but fair. He said how you asked his dad at a baseball game if you could pick him up for church and he agreed. He said you took him to church in a white bus and even led him to the Lord."

"I'm surprised to hear that, but then again, he's one to hide his emotions and keep his thoughts to himself. You may have noticed that now and then, haven't you Brisk?" he said with a smile.

"Oh, yes. That's an accurate description of him."

"That's all he said about the baseball game?"

"That's all, why, is there more?"

"Yes, a lot more. I didn't know him, but I saw the pain in him, physical and psychological. His father beat him that day before the game. I remember his ear was bloody. I saw the injury, but he was too afraid to answer my questions. So I went over and told his father two things: stop the abuse and let me take him to church, or else. That's how he started going to church. Follow me back to Mountain Springs, okay?"

"Yes, and ah, thanks, John."

Trooper Allen drove off and Brisk followed in Lake's Jeep. On the warm dirty sidewalk, the remains of two ice cream cones melted while in the western horizon the earlier brilliant colors of the sunset faded to dull dark grays.

John pulled his cruiser into the courthouse parking lot in Mountain Springs just after 10:00 p.m. Brisk was right behind him and Kenzie was standing there waiting.

Just as John got out of the car Kenzie, visibly upset, walked right up to him, and said, "Couldn't this have waited, John? I mean, we just had a funeral. What were you thinking?"

"Mackenzie," John began with a stern voice "It wasn't up to me. I'm only here because I wanted to help your brother not hurt him. I didn't have to go to Round Island to pick him up. Trooper Bauer could have accomplished that on his own. I asked to go because I cared about Lake. Now act like a sensible man and help us out. If you can't do that then I want you to go home, do you understand?"

"But, John, he's beat! Couldn't you wait?"

"No, it was not up to me. Now act like a sensible man, do you understand, Mackenzie?"

"Yes, sir. I'm sorry."

Trooper Bauer pulled an exhausted Lake out of the cruiser. As soon as Lake saw Kenzie he began yelling. "Mackenzie! Look, I've got handcuffs on. Your dad was right. I'm just a worthless punk. He said I'd probably end up in jail someday, and he was right! He was right about everything!"

John walked over to Lake and face-to-face he said, "I want you to shut up right now."

Lake said, "Don't worry. You won't have to listen to my voice ever again. I won't waste your time. I apparently wasted it for the last eighteen years."

"Take him inside," John told Trooper Bauer.

After everyone was inside the district justice entered the room. "Please be seated," he said.

"What are the charges, Officer?"

"Assault and battery, terroristic threats, breaking and entering, trespassing, receiving stolen property, and concealing a deadly weapon, your Honor."

"Lakeland Nidhatak, will you please stand and state 'guilty or not guilty'?" Lake was nearly asleep and didn't respond. "Is he drunk, Officer? I don't have sympathy for a drunkard in my courtroom."

"No, he's not drunk, Your Honor." Trooper Bauer said. "I'm told he is physically exhausted. Apparently not eating or sleeping for several days and...his father funeral was today."

"Why would you bring him in here under those circumstances?"

"Charges were pressed this morning and we just located him in Round Island this evening. The seriousness of the charges warranted us to bring him in."

"The charges are serious. Bail is set at $50,000. Anyone here to post bail?"

"Mackenzie?" John asked.

"I don't have that kind of money, I'm sorry. Can Lake use the Eddy?" Kenzie asked.

"I'm afraid he's in no condition to do that and probably won't cooperate."

"Very well," the district justice said. "He can sleep off whatever his problem is in jail tonight, and we'll take it up in the morning, 9:00 a.m. Good night."

Everyone stood up as the district justice left the room, except Lake. John and a sheriff deputy each grabbed one of Lake's arms and took him to one of the two prison cells the small county had. As they placed Lake on the bed, John turned to the deputy. "Can you give me a few minutes with him?" The deputy stepped out of the cell and John knelt down along the side of the bed. "Lakeland, this night pains me greatly. It tears my heart to see you in here. You got to take control of yourself. You've had enough lately, but you are a soldier of our Lord Jesus. Give it all to him and continue to be a testimony. Can you hear me? Lake?" John pushed back Lake's hair from his face. Placing his hand on Lake's forehead, he prayed, "Father, heal my son of all his emotional pain, evaporate all those scars on his soul. Use him mightily for your glory, in Jesus's name. Amen." John stood up and wiped a tear from his eye. Then he reached down and touched Lake's forehead again. "Your forehead is hot, you must have a fever." He turned and walked out of the cell. "God, help him, please," he whispered softly.

The deputy saw John and walked to the cell and closed the door, something John couldn't bring himself to do. "He seems to have a fever so watch him for me, okay? Any problems call the barracks and have them call me. See you in the morning."

John and Trooper Bauer came out of the courthouse. Trooper Bauer walked over to the patrol car and got in. John continued to where Brisk and Kenzie were sitting on a bench. They stood up but said nothing. He looked at them and said, "He'll be fine, we'll come back in the morning, and he'll be rested, and hopefully, the district justice will be in a better mood. He'll set a court date, and we'll see what happens. So go home and get some sleep. Okay?"

"John," Brisk began, "I can't believe he's going to spend the night in jail. It pains me to leave him here. A few hours ago he went from being knocked down, beaten emotionally to being on top of the world. You should have seen him. He saw that race and said he felt God wanted him to do it. He missed the start and still won. Kenzie, remember when we did that midnight run and Lawrence told Lake about that runner in the Boston marathon being led in by the police cars? Lake said that will never happen, but it did today, for four whole miles! He suddenly realized God did it just to display his love to Lake. He was euphoric! We enjoyed the hot summer night, the sunset, the trail birds—"

"The trail birds," Kenzie interrupted with a smile.

"But then, all this had to happen."

"God's love is awesome, unimaginable, impossible for us to fathom," John said. "Pray that God will use this for all of us to grow in him, to see and know his love."

"Ah, John, I'm sorry about earlier. I really am. You've always treated Lake and I decently, giving us more respect and love than from... I got to get home. Good night, John."

"Sit down, Mackenzie. Let's pray. Oh, gracious God. Trouble builds character and faith. I pray for the hidden strengths in Mackenzie that I've seen for years to come forth according to your will. And I pray for Brisk to gently guide both Lakeland and Mackenzie through any emotional turmoil the next few days. If they lose even a little sight of you, may she put them back on track with prayer and scripture, allowing your love to flow through her to these sons of yours. In Jesus's name. Amen."

"Thanks, John, you sure can pray," Kenzie said. "Hey, could we all meet for breakfast at the Eddy, about eight?"

"That's fine," John said.

"Good idea, Kenzie," Brisk replied. "Are your…are your…"

"Is Llewellyn and Lydia, my brother and sister, there? Yes. We had a great discussion. They are Christians and musicians. You got to meet them. They are wonderful. Well, let's head out. Good night, John, and thanks."

"Thank you, John, bless you," Brisk said as Kenzie and her began walking to the parking lot. After a few feet, Kenzie turned around and walked back to John and gave him a hug. John looked at him. "As Lakeland always says, 'Life is hard, but God is good, and the best is yet to come.' Remember that."

Kenzie, with tears in his eyes, nodded his head in affirmation, and then hugged John again. He turned and began walking away and then looked back and waved at John. John, standing under a park light, waved back and watched them get in their Jeeps and leave. He turned to look at the courthouse. "Good night, Lakeland. I'll be back in the morning. God will take care of you. Lord, please give him a good night's rest. He has a lot ahead him in the next few weeks." He got into the patrol car and drove away into the night.

*****

Just after midnight, Lake awoke. "Oh," he moaned, holding his head. The moon was shining through a small window, and as he slowly sat up, it began lighting up half his sweating face. He stood up slowly; looking around the room he softly said, "I'm in jail. I'm really in jail." He walked to the window and looked out through the bars. "Oh, God, such a beautiful night. I want to be out there so bad. What have I done? I'll be out at the knoll the next full moon. I'll be praising you, Lord, because I know you'll get me out of this mess. Lord, I want to be out there right now. I'm so sorry I disappointed you…again. But I see the moon. I know you're with me." He began to sing softly:

How long until I see the One that gave life to me
Even then You'll be too beautiful for my human eyes
With Your arms of love I'll be lifted from Your feet
As Your radiance evaporates my pool of tears away
How long 'til I thank the Son who came to set me free
How long 'til I kiss the Man crushed at Gethsemane
How long 'til I worship the Lamb slain on Calvary
'til I gaze upon the risen One, behold the face of the glorified Son
How long, Jesus, 'til I see the One who gave life to me.

Lake quickly sat down on the bed. "I'm sorry, Lord, I've got to sit down."

"What are you singing over there?" a voice whispered.

"I'm sorry if I disturbed you, I thought I was alone," Lake replied.

"They brought me in a while ago. Maybe I disturbed you," the man said.

"I don't remember," Lake told him. "Doesn't matter. Anyway, my name is Lake. What's your name?"

"Lou," he replied. "That was a nice song you sang. You really believe in God, don't you?"

"Wait a second. I don't feel so good. Awl," Lake moaned as he sat on the floor resting his back again the cell wall. "No, I don't believe. I know. I know for a fact God is real. I know for sure he loves you. Have you ever given him a chance?"

"Let me ask you something. Why are you in jail?"

"Oh, I punched a pastor."

He started to laugh then asked, "How can you tell me to believe when you punched a pastor, one of your own. What kind of testimony is that?

"Not a good testimony. He said some terrible things about my brother and I, I just lost it. He was so mean. I wish I could say I'm sorry, but I'm not. Christians can be worse than non-Christians, and I guess I'm not a good example."

"I'd like to punch a few Christians," Lou told him.

"Christians will let you down. So don't follow any."

"What?" Lou asked.

"Don't follow a Christian, follow Jesus. Christians can be examples, but we will let you down. Follow the perfect one, Jesus."

"So you're a Christian?"

"Yes, I told you that."

"Then why'd you punch the pastor?"

"I told you. Why are you in here?"

"Public drunkenness. I'm a twenty-five-year-old alcoholic."

"Oh, you're a drunk?"

"No. I'm not a drunk. I'm an alcoholic."

"Same thing!"

"No, it's not."

"Then tell me the difference."

"Well, a drunk is, ah, a drunk is, well, an alcoholic is…look, I know you're right. It is the same thing."

"My dad is a drunk. I mean he was. Alcohol destroyed our family. We lost everything because of it. Even lost our home and had to move thousands of miles away. It still hurts. Until you admit it's destroying you, you'll never be a real man. You'll never be the real man God designed you to be."

"That's what my wife says. Hey, what did you mean when you said your dad was an alcoholic?"

THE RACE

Looking up at the clock in the hallway, Lake replied, "His funeral was yesterday, I think."

"You punched the pastor at your father's funeral?"

"No, no, no. Different pastor, different day. I punched this one after church Sunday."

"Why are you staring out the window?"

"It's the moon. It's so beautiful. When I see the moon, I believe God is near to me. I mean, he's always near, it's just extra special." Lake pulled a chair up to the window and unsteadily stepped up to look out. "Lou. This is a divine appointment God set up between you and me. He wants you. He's calling your name."

"You really believe all that?"

"I know it. Plus, I bet your wife is praying for you right now."

Lake could see tears in Lou's eyes in the cell's faint light. "Lou, do you want to pray with me? Do you want to be one of God's men? Do you want to be your wife's dream man?"

"Yeah. I do."

Lake stepped down and reached through the bars. "Give me your hand." As Lou held onto Lake's hand, Lake began to pray, "Father, I never expected to be in jail. I deserve it. I shouldn't have hit Pastor Avalon, but it sure felt good. Oh, I'm sorry. I shouldn't have said that. Convict my heart. But most importantly, I want to pray for Lou, not me." Whispering to Lou, Lake said, "I'm sorry, Lou, I should have prayed for you first instead of myself. See, I screwed up already. I'm sorry. But God understands. I always mess up. Anyway, God, I believe this is a divine appointment. I pray you open up Lou's eyes and heart to you. Give him peace that passes all understanding. Help him to be the man you want him to be and the man his wife knows he could be. Help us to make it through this night."

"Oh, and I lift up those around the world suffering for you, the persecuted church. I pray for strength and courage for those suffering for the cause of Jesus.

"I especially pray for those in prison tonight, Lord. I think I can understand, at least a little. Give them peace to endure. You are with them. Blessings to my friends too.

"Now, Lou, I want you to repeat after me, okay?"

"Okay," Lou softly answered.

"Father God, I want the true wine only you can give."

"Father God, I want the true wine only you can give."

"I want to drink from the well where I'll never thirst again."

"I want to drink from the well where I'll never thirst again."

"I want Jesus in my heart."

"I want Jesus in my heart."

"I believe you are in my heart."

"I believe you are in my heart."

"And I can't wait to tell my wife!"

Lou smiled widely. "And I can't wait to tell my wife!"

Lake's grip tightened as he said, "Welcome, brother."

"I feel different already," Lou joyfully told Lake. "I really do! You're really genuine, aren't you?"

"A genuine screw up, maybe. But God uses even screw ups like me. Read the Word, the Bible. It's nourishment for your spirit. Read with your wife. I guarantee your marriage will be renewed. You'll be living as God purposed."

"Thanks, Lake."

"Lou, look! The moon is shining right on us! His love always shines on us. But as I said before, when I see the moonlight, I imagine his love coming right down on me. No love is greater."

"Will you sing that song again?" Lou asked.

"Oh, I can't sing. I really don't feel very well at all. I feel like I'm burning up actually."

"Please," Lou asked.

Lake sat on the floor again, his back against his cot so he could face Lou's cell. "Okay, here goes…"

> How long until I see the One that gave life to me
> Even then You'll be too beautiful for my human eyes
> With Your arms of love I'll be lifted from Your feet

As Your radiance evaporates…evaporates…
evap…

"Lake?" Lou whispered. "Lake? Are you okay? Lake? Lake!"
Lou stood up and looked down the hallway. "Guard! Help! We need help!"

11

Forgiveness

The next morning, Kenzie was up early and sitting on the porch of the Eddy when Brisk arrived. "Good morning, Brisk. You're up early."

"Good morning, Kenzie. I couldn't sleep knowing Lake was in jail. It broke my heart thinking of him staying there overnight," she said as she said down on one of the rockers next to Kenzie.

"I know how you feel," he said as he reached up and held her hand. "And all because of Avalon. It just pisses me off. Where's forgiveness at? Where's understanding? Where's brotherhood? Christians!"

"You sound just like your brother," she said with a slight smile. "Lydia and Llewellyn still sleeping?"

"I just put the coffee on and woke them up. I didn't get to talk to them last night so they have no idea what's going on."

"Hey, here comes John. He's early too. Didn't anyone sleep last night?"

John pulled his pickup truck in front of the Eddy. "Good morning, Kenzie, Brisk," he said as he got out and walked to the porch.

"Morning, John, everything okay?" Kenzie asked.

John sat down on the steps and turned to Kenzie and Brisk. "Now before you get upset, everything is fine. Do you understand?"

"No!" Kenzie said as he stood up. "What's wrong now?"

"Lake was taken to the hospital early this morning, but he's fine. He was unresponsive when the deputy sheriff checked on him.

They called me, and I went right out early this morning. He's had a bad case of heat exhaustion. The doctor was concerned he had heat stroke, but that was ruled out. As you know, he hasn't slept much and hasn't eaten much. That race yesterday was too much for his body, and he is suffering the consequences."

"Plus the funeral," Brisk added as she stood up and held Kenzie hand.

"That's right. All those things together were too much for his system. We all have limits."

"Why didn't you call me?" Kenzie asked.

"Because the doctor said he would be fine and needed to rest. And I know you needed to rest. If it was life-threatening, I would have called you, Kenzie."

"He was a little forgetful after the race and had a bad headache," Brisk told them. "I wish I had realized what was happening to him. I asked him if he was all right and he said he was. I should have known. We were having such a great time until…"

"Until I showed up?" John asked.

"Well, yes. I'm sorry."

"It's okay, I know what you mean."

"Well, let's go to the hospital," Kenzie said anxiously.

"No, we're having breakfast," John said as he stood up. Doctor will be checking on Lake about nine, and he said to stop out at ten. That's gives us plenty of time to eat and fellowship. I hear you're a good cook, Kenzie."

"What about the district justice hearing? That was at nine?" Kenzie asked.

"The district justice has been notified and the hearing has been delayed until further notice."

"Why are you always so calm and collective?" Kenzie asked John with a smile.

"It's called peace. God is our peace," John answered.

"You're such a cool guy, John. Sometimes I wish… I wish…"

"Wish what, Kenzie?' Brisk asked as they all began walking toward the front door.

"Nothing. I'm just tired," he said softly.

"Brisk turned and winked at John who nodded and smiled.

John and Brisk sat down at one of the tables while Kenzie turned up the flame on the grill. "That'll take a few minutes to heat up," he said as he sat down at the table. Just then Llewellyn and Lydia came out of the bunkrooms. "Good morning, everyone," Llewellyn said.

"Good morning," Kenzie, John, and Brisk responded.

"You awake, Lydia?" Kenzie asked.

She smiled and nodded her head. "I slept like a baby," she said softly.

Kenzie got up. "Coffee's ready. I'll bring the pot over."

"I'll help you with the cups," Llewellyn told him.

After everyone was seated, Kenzie asked, "What would everyone like for breakfast? The special is pancakes, turkey bacon, and mandarin oranges."

"What else is on the menu?" John asked.

"Let me think. Now I'm pretending I'm Lake."

"I thought you were up to something," Brisk said.

"What else is on the menu? Well, I have pancakes, turkey bacon, and mandarin oranges, and pancakes, turkey bacon, and mandarin oranges, or we also have pancakes, turkey bacon, and mandarin oranges."

Everyone was laughing.

"What would you like, madam?" Kenzie said to Lydia.

"I decided on the special, please."

"Thank you, madam."

"Monsieur, what would you like to order, please," Kenzie asked Llewellyn.

"I guess I'll have the special. Um, where is Lake?" he asked.

"Oh, he's in slammer," Kenzie answered.

"What?" Llewellyn asked with a startled look.

"He's in the big house."

"Do you mean he's in jail? For what?"

"Oh, he punched the pastor," Kenzie said then started laughing.

"Kenzie. It's not funny," Brisk said as she began to laugh.

"It is funny. He does the craziest things. Nobody punches the pastor."

John put his head down, trying desperately not to join the laughing.

"John, are you laughing?" Kenzie asked, trying to get John to look up.

"Kenzie! Stop it. It's not funny," Brisk said while trying to stop laughing.

"Actually, Llewellyn, he's in the hospital right now," Kenzie told him.

"Come on. Are you serious?" Lydia asked.

"Oh, yeah. He's in the hospital. But as soon as he's released, again, as soon as he's released its back to jail."

"Why does he have to go back to jail?"

Kenzie's face changed suddenly to a serious look, then he yelled, "Because I have no money to get him out!" Tears rushed to his eyes. "I'm sorry. I'm so sorry." He was filling a coffee mug, and not realizing it, the mug was overflowing. Brisk grabbed Kenzie's arm and pulled up the coffeepot. Everyone took napkins and began cleaning up the coffee.

"I'm sorry, everyone," Kenzie said softly. "Wow, what happened to our happy world all of a sudden? We always had trouble with dad, but Lake and I were so blessed by our friends, our church, just a good life. Now it seems it all collapsed. I don't understand it."

"Kenzie," John began, "it didn't collapse. It's just the normal Christian life. God hasn't left us. He's right on the same throne he was on yesterday. He's still in charge. Death, sickness, troubles are all around. They are a part of life, a part of growing up. Lake will be fine. You will be fine. Life will go on.

"You have good grades at college, a good relationship with the Lord, a beautiful fiancé, a good brother. This is life, Kenzie, the normal Christian life. We don't enjoy seeing others suffer, die, or have troubles. We, as Christians, have the ability to give it to the Lord and be at peace. He never will leave us nor forsake us. God is love. What you are feeling for your brother is love. Be at peace, Kenzie."

"Thanks, John," Kenzie replied, and he smiled. "You always know what to say. I'll get breakfast."

At 10:00 a.m., John, Kenzie, Brisk, Lydia and Llewellyn arrived at the hospital. When they walked in Lake's room, he was on the phone and watching TV. When he saw the group, he signaled them to be quiet and pointed to the TV.

"It's Avalon," Lake whispered. "He's a guest on this call in this Christian talk show. He's telling about his book *Forgiveness*! Can you believe it! I was so mad I threw my bedpan and dented the wall!"

"I hope it was empty!" Kenzie seriously asked.

"Kenzie, I'd use the window before I'd use a bedpan."

"Well, you sound back to normal," John said as everyone laughed.

"Shhh! Their phone is ringing. Please be me."

"Hello," the narrator on TV said. "Who do we have on the phone, and what question do you have for Pastor Avalon?"

"It's me," Lake whispered to the group. "Hello," he said into the phone. "I'm Noah Buddy," he told the host and then whispered to the group, "Noah, buddy, nobody, get it?" John shook his head and everyone giggled.

"What is your question, Noah?" the host asked.

"Yes, sir. How often should I forgive?" Lake asked.

"Seventy times seventy," Pastor Avalon answered.

"Have you forgiven everyone that has offended you, Mr. Avalon?" Lake asked.

"That's Pastor Avalon, and yes, I have forgiven everyone. If I didn't forgive, I wouldn't be perfect."

Lake rolled his eyes. "Well, I know this guy who had a conflict with his pastor and the pastor pressed erroneous charges against him. Is that right to do? I mean, where is the forgiveness, Mr. Avalon?" Lake prodded.

"That's Pastor Avalon. Anyway, no matter how severe the offense, there must be forgiveness. I think the pastor you mentioned should lead an example and forgive. Certainly I would have without a second thought."

"Isn't it true, Mr. Avalon, that you insulted someone, he hit you, and you had that person arrested and added many false charges?" Lake asked.

"No, I would never do such a thing. Never."

"Does that answer your questions, Noah?" the host asked.

"Will you ask Mr. Avalon what he intends to do after having Lakeland Nidhatak arrested yesterday?" Lake asked the host.

"You had someone arrested and you are selling a book about forgiveness?" the host asked a visibly upset Avalon.

"I think this is a prank call," Avalon suggested.

"Noah, is this Lakeland a friend of yours?" the host asked.

"Yes, and he's right here. Do you want to talk to him?"

"Yes!" the host replied.

Lake switched the phone from one ear to the other and deepened his voice. The group shook their heads in amazement. "Good morning, this is Lakeland Nidhatak."

"Good morning," the host said. "Where are you calling from?"

"The hospital," Lake replied.

"Please hang up on this hippie boy!" Avalon demanded.

"Let me ask Lakeland his side of the story," the host told Avalon. "First, why are you in the hospital, Lakeland?"

"Well, I haven't slept for days. My dad's funeral was yesterday. Then I ran this race, and I remarkably won. God was showering me with his love. Then I was arrested because of Avalon and put in jail. I was having heat exhaustion overnight and here I am. The real root of all of this is that Avalon insulted my brother last Sunday, and I hit him. He saw my bloody beaten brother a week earlier along the road and just drove by, judging. I know a lot about Avalon because that's all he talks about, himself. You may have noticed. Where is his forgiveness? I forgive him. What's a hippie?"

"Your reply, Pastor Avalon?" the host inquired. Avalon stood up and walked off the stage. The host and a cameraman followed him off the stage and stopped him outside the building as he approached his car. "Pastor Avalon, why are you upset? Is all this true?"

"This is a personal matter. It has nothing to do with my pastoral calling or my professional writings. It's totally personal," Avalon nervously replied.

"Are you going to forgive Lakeland?" the host asked as Avalon got into his car. Avalon didn't reply but sped out of the parking lot.

"Well, everyone," the host began, "you've been watching an unrepentant Pastor Avalon refusing to forgive someone while promoting his book *Forgiveness*. While we don't condone what Lakeland did, Pastor Avalon lost a great opportunity for restoration between two brothers in the Lord. Wow, I don't know what to say. We'll certainly check into the story and report back tomorrow morning. Perhaps Pastor Avalon will have a change of heart."

"Thank you, Lakeland and Noah, for calling in. We hope to be talking to you later today. Now it's time for a commercial, we'll be right back with another guest."

Lake hung up the phone, turned off the TV, and began grinning widely.

"You are one crazy bastard," Kenzie told him.

"You certainly got guts," Llewellyn said shaking his head.

"Lakeland, do you forgive Avalon?" John asked.

"Completely," Lake replied firmly. "I didn't plan on seeing him on TV but right there he was. Maybe we had a divine appointment. But I do feel bad for him. It's like he can't see the forest for the trees, but I think he really is trying. I just don't understand. But I do forgive him.

"How are you feeling?" Brisk asked Lake as she held his hand and felt his forehead.

"Better. I feel tired but a lot better," he replied.

"Kenzie made us a great breakfast this morning," Lydia told Lake.

"It was great. We had the special," Llewellyn added.

"Oh, the special. Kenzie was making fun of me wasn't he?"

"No comment," Brisk answered with a smile.

"What did the doctor say when he checked you this morning," John asked.

"What all doctors tell me."

"What's that?" Brisk wondered.

"It's all in my head."

As everyone began laughing a nurse came into the room. "Lakeland, you can be discharged from the hospital as soon as you get dressed."

"Thank you," Lake replied as the nurse left the room. "Guess I have to go back to jail. I don't want to go back to jail. It was nice to relax and laugh with you all for a few minutes and forget life's problems."

John cell phone rang. He walked into the hall so he could hear better.

"Lake, can't you use the Eddy to post bail?" Kenzie asked.

"I could, but it's just not fair. Avalon! Why can people be so mean, especially some Christians?

John quickly came back into the room, smiling. "Lake, that was Trooper Bauer. Avalon called him and dropped all the charges. He left no explanation. You can go home."

Llewellyn recited a verse: "Lake, remember Romans 8:28: 'For God works all things together for good to those who love him and are called according to his purpose.'"

"Wow. He did have a change of heart," Lake said softly. "Maybe I should call him and see if he's okay?"

"Big bro, let's just go home," Kenzie said seriously. "Let's have a mellow afternoon and ponder the last few days. Just you and me for a few hours. I think we need that."

"Yeah," Lake answered. "You're right. We need that."

"We can hike the Sheba Trail, sit below the cross, and talk. Everyone can join us at the Eddy for a cookout later tonight," Kenzie suggested.

"That sounds sweet."

"Lydia and Llewellyn are leaving tomorrow morning so we can have the cookout in their honor," Kenzie suggested.

"Yeah, they've been through enough just meeting us the last few days. Okay, everyone out so I can get dressed and we can get out of here."

"Here's some clean clothes," Kenzie said as he handed them to Lake.

"Thanks."

Everyone left the room as Lake got dressed. "God," he began praying, "I just want a normal life. A normal Christian life. I'm sorry, I'm tired. God, help Avalon. Help Lou. I'll feel better tomorrow.

Thank you for getting me out of another mess. Let's go home. I just want to go home."

John opened the door. "Are you all right, Lake?"

Yeah, I'm fine. Just talking to our Father."

"Lake, I have some news from church. Pastor Bentley resigned."

"Because of all the trouble I caused! Right?"

"No, no, no. He was away to interview at several churches in the southern tier and accepted a job offer. It had nothing to do with you."

"That's a relief, though I'm sad to lose him."

"Well, the bad news is that Justin blames you and is furious. I tried intervening, but he wouldn't listen to me nor Pastor Bentley. You know he's been in and out of drug rehab. I've been counseling him for a few years. I love the kid, but he is so messed up, he breaks my heart. He just can't seem to stay clean and get on with his life. So avoid him if you can. If he gives you any trouble, give me a call."

"Yeah, um, John, I'm so sorry about getting angry with you at Round Island. You are my mentor, my friend. I'm sorry for what I said yesterday. I never told you this before, but wish you were my dad."

John looked at Lake and gave a proud smile. "Lake," he said as he placed his arm around Lake's shoulder and led him toward the door. "Let's go home."

Lake smiled back as he placed his arm on John's shoulder. "Yeah, let's go home."

12

He Restores

Several weeks had passed, and it was now mid-August. Lake, Kenzie, Lawrence, and Parker just returned from a week backpacking the Susquehannock Trail in northern Pennsylvania.

"Grab your backpacks and put them on the porch of the Eddy," Lake told the others. "If you want, pile your dirty clothes and I'll wash them."

"Where do you want the tents set up to dry, Lake?" Lawrence asked.

"Right there in the grass between the Base Camp and the Eddy," Lake answered.

After the tents were set up, the gear cleaned, and the laundry was in the washer the four sat out on the Eddy's porch, each drinking a soda and reminiscing.

"That was a great trip," Parker signed.

"I can't believe I finally saw a Pennsylvania elk!" Lawrence exclaimed. "They were huge and beautiful!"

"I think we saw four elk, one being a bull," Kenzie said. "Plus, four rattlesnakes, plenty of deer, two hawk, and one bald eagle. No humanoids. It was a wild adventure, Lake. Thank you."

"Yeah. Thanks, Lake," Lawrence added. "That was tough but so worth it. I can't believe you did several trips that lasted months. That's crazy."

"It really takes a few weeks to adjust to the any new routine. After two weeks, your legs get strong, and hiking is so much easier," Lake told them. "Plus, after a few weeks, you start loving your new home in the woods."

"You did the Appalachian Trail, the Pacific Crest Trail, and the Continental Divide Trail?" Lawrence asked.

"Lake's a Triple Crowner," Kenzie said proudly.

"What's that?"

"It's when you've hiked the big three trails. The AT, the PCT and the CDT," Kenzie explained.

"Not a big deal," Lake told them. "If I can do it, anyone could do it. Hey, let's get everything set up for tonight. It's the Judah Lions plus Lydia, Llewellyn, and John are coming also."

"Lake," Kenzie began, "as I said when we were on the Susquehannock, you seem changed. I mean, when you got out of the, the—"

"The slammer is what you called it," Lake interjected.

"Well, yeah, that place. You seemed so withdrawn from everyone and everything. But just before our hike you seemed different, so confident. You were so happy, and we had such a good time. You forgave everyone, didn't you?"

"First of all, I feel at home on the trail, in the woods. And of course, I forgave everyone. I did a lone hike one evening and I forgave, especially the one I needed to forgive the most."

"Dad? He's the one you needed to forgive most."

"No. Not him. Someone else."

"Who?"

"I'll tell you later. For now, let's get everything ready for tonight."

"Most of the instruments are on the stage in the Eddy. What else do we need to do?" Lawrence asked.

"Not the Eddy. No. Not the Eddy. The Treehouse."

"The Treehouse!" Kenzie said, wide eyed.

"I didn't know you had a treehouse!" Lawrence added.

"It's one of his many secrets," Kenzie explained. "No one has been to the Treehouse. Even I am not allowed there."

"Like that has stopped you," Lake told him as he smiled.

"I guess I am an explorer like my big brother."

"Exploring and snooping are two different things."

"It's the same so, shut up!"

"Okay, seriously. We are going to the Treehouse. We need our backpacks to transport everything up. Oh, take the old instruments because it may rain tonight. We'll have a fire going and we'll make pizza mountain pies. John is going to give a short message and then we'll just worship. Geradine is going to sing tonight. Then, we'll pray for the church, for forgiveness, for each other."

"Lake! Geradine? Are you sure?" a surprise Kenzie asked.

"Yes. I am sure."

"Sound good, Lake," Parker signed. "Who's Geradine?"

"She lives in the Treehouse."

"Okay. A lady lives in the treehouse," Lawrence said sarcastically. "I don't want to know anymore. So how do we get to this secret treehouse, Lake?" Lawrence asked.

"Follow the Secret Trail?"

"Where's that?"

"Can't tell you. It's a secret!" Lake said, laughing. "Follow me."

Brisk, Brandy, Zachariah, Llewelyn, Lydia, and John arrived at the Eddy around 6:00 p.m. Everyone was talking as they sat on the porch of the Eddy. Everyone listened as Lake, Kenzie, Lawrence, and Parker told them about their backpacking trip on the Susquehannock Trail.

Lake got Brisk's attention and asked her to walk to the cross on the Sheba Trail. They walked down the trail, crossed the creek, and then walked up the knoll to the cross. A warm breeze was blowing the tree branches as the creek sang softly below them.

Once they got there, Lake looked away from her then asked, "Brisk, I just need to know this: why did you hit me after we left North Mountain Christian Center?"

"Lake, I am so, so sorry. I have no excuse to give you," she said as she walked over behind him and placed her arms around him. "I was wondering if and when you would mention it to me. You don't know how sorry I am, Lake."

"Can you possibly understand how I felt at that moment?" he asked her. "I was starting to like you and then you did that. I gave up on you right then and there. I even said to God something like 'Lost another one.' It placed another painful twist in an already twisted heart."

"I thought you had forgiven me because we had such a good time at Round Island."

"I did forgive you. But I am so afraid you'll get mad at me and do it again. I couldn't bare it again, not from anyone. Especially not from you. How can I know you won't do that?"

"Lake, turn around and look at me. Turn around please." After he turned around, she looked directly at him. "Lake, I slapped you because I thought you slept with Marilyn. I was so upset when I heard that. I kept it inside of me. I should have confronted you as soon as I heard. You probably would have told me the truth, wouldn't you?"

"Why wouldn't I? I mean, this isn't a soap opera, and it's not ratings week. It's life. If we can't be simply honest and open to each other…what am I saying. I guess it was my fault for not opening up more to people. I was just being and doing things I like to do, enjoying the outdoors and sharing the love of Jesus. I didn't think I had to tell anyone what I do. I've really had no one to share my adventures with until Kenzie came back to Mountain Springs. My dad never wanted to hear about anything I did. I'd find something really cool out exploring and come home excited to tell him, but he'd just tell me to shut up. I learned early in life to keep my mouth shut. I think no one is interested in my adventures."

"I always will want to hear about your adventures, Lake. You haven't told me much but what you have told me thrills my heart. You are the number one explorer in my life.

"Lake, did you have this talk with Lawrence, about forgiveness?" Brisk asked.

"No, why?"

"Well, he punched you a few times for starters."

"So? We fought before. I'd kick his butt, and he knows it. But that day at church, I soon understood where he was coming from before I even left him. He cared about you and didn't want you hurt. Plus, as we now know, he still had feeling for Marilyn. I just needed him at that time and knew he wouldn't be interested in talking so I left. Parker was just listening to his big brother. Brandy and Zackary didn't know it was going to happen. I wasn't mad at any of them, just..."

"Just what, Lake?"

"Disappointed."

"Disappointed because no one stood up for you?"

"No. Disappointed they should have gone back in church and started playing, or at least in the parking lot. People would have stood with them, and it would have been a special time of worship."

"You weren't there when they were kicked out, so they didn't have anyone to tell them what to do," Brisk told him.

"Lawrence is a leader. He just doesn't know it. You wouldn't have wanted me to tell them what to do that day or else Avalon and Bentley would each be wearing a guitar over their heads."

"He did lead well when we were looking for you. He took charge in directing us and praying. He said he had a good teacher."

"Who?"

"Well, you Lakeland Nidhatak. Who else?"

"Me?"

"Yes, you. When he said that he got teary eyed. He was genuinely worried about you."

"Um, so, are you ready for tonight?"

"Yes, Lake, I'm ready. What did you do to get ready?"

"You really want to know?"

"Yes."

"Well, I went out to what I call the Secret Knoll at the Secret Pond.'"

"Are you going to take me there someday?"

"It wouldn't be a secret then. Why does everyone want to know my secrets? Anyway, I went out there and sat down looking over the pond. I wrote down everything and everyone I needed to forgive, and I forgave it or forgave them. I prayed first. But when I read down the list the hardest thing was last, and I only wrote that as an afterthought. But when I read through them all, I was fine, until the last one."

"What was it, Lake?"

"It was 'forgive me.' I started crying. I never realized that was a problem. I must have been blaming me for everything. Maybe that's why I hated me. I asked God's help in forgiving myself."

"Did you forgive yourself?"

"By faith, yes. I handed it all to him. Not my problem anymore. Then I burnt the paper. Hey, it's almost time for the service to start, we've better head back."

Back at Base Camp, Lake addressed everyone as some sat on the Eddy's porch, and some sat in the grass. "Thanks for everyone coming tonight. Regarding the big race everyone knows that Llewellyn and I are doing the ultra. As for the relay, there are several changes with the relay team. Lydia is going to run and as well as a young runner I met the Round Island race a few months ago."

"Benjamin?" Brisk asked. "The guy you gave your trophy to?"

"Yeah, Benjamin. He's been practicing hard since that race and called to see if he could run with us. I told him about the hundred-mile relay and he was so excited when I asked him to join the team.

"So the relay breaks the one hundred miles into twelve sections. With two additional runners that means four of you will need to run twice and four of you only need to run once. Check the roster and see if you approve of the changes I made. We can move anyone around if need be, except for Lawrence and Kenzie. I assigned steepest and most rugged sections to them because they are the power machines for the hills.

"As for tonight, we want this to be a time of seeking the Lord, seeking forgiveness, praying for the church, praying for the persecuted church. We want to pray for direction of the band. We want to pray for safety at the race. We want to pray for the wedding. We want to pray for divine appointments. We need to pray for leadership for North Brook. Any questions or comments?"

John spoke up. "Well, everyone. Just so you know, I've been asked to fill in as interim pastor until a permanent pastor can be found."

Everyone applauded and shouted. Lake and Kenzie looked at each other with wide-eyed and mouths dropped.

"Well, John, that's great news. I think you teach great at your Bible study. I can't wait to hear you preach in church. God is good!"

"I'll try my best," John said humbly.

"What a great way to start the night. Grab the food and let's go to the Treehouse!"

"To the Treehouse!" everyone shouted in unison. A single file of talking and laughing hikers went up the driveway and turned onto the Secret Trail.

At the Treehouse, Brisk, Brandy, Zachariah, Llewelyn, Lydia, and John looked around in amazement. "What a beautiful hideaway, Lake," Brisk told him. "Beautiful."

"Yes, Lakeland. Absolutely beautiful! Brandy told him."

Tall rhododendrons and mountain laurel camouflaged the site. There was a firepit with benches and folding chairs around it. The Treehouse overlooked the firepit at thirty feet away.

"So that's the Treehouse," John said. "How far can you see from up there, Lake?"

"You can see all the way into Mountain Springs. You can see the state forests in the other directions. At night, you can see the lights of Thorndale, fifty miles away," Lake him. "And that's just the first floor. On the roof you can see over seventy-five miles in each direction. Sometimes I lay on my back up there and watch the stars and pray. This is my prayer closet, I guess."

"What's that on the first floor under a tarp?" Zachariah asked.

"That's Geraldine. She might sing this evening, Lord willing. I removed the tarps I had on all four sides of the Treehouse so she'd have no obstructions."

"What are you up to Lake?" Brisk asked.

"Trust me, as I am trusting the Lord. The is a leviathan step of faith."

"Leviathan?" she asked?

As everyone took a chair, Lake began speaking as he lit the fire and constantly watched the flames, adjusting the wood to burn sufficiently for the mountain pies. "Again, I am glad all of you were able to be here tonight. Let's pray. Let's pray, not looking at our feet but looking toward the woods or the sky, taking in his creativity.

"Father, blessed be your name. Tonight, we seek you, asking direction for every one of us. We pray for the persecuted church. They ask not that the persecution to stop but to be able to endure the persecution, to have complete confidence in your Word. We especially pray for John as he temporarily leads North Brook. We want what you want. We are at war with the enemy. We are warriors, give us leaders and make us stronger. All for you. Everyone…"

"All for you," everyone repeated.

John began his message: "A few years ago, at an Easter sunrise service held at the hill looking over Mountain Springs, Lakeland Nidhatak gave a short message. Considering all that has transpired over the last two months, I think it is appropriate to repeat it tonight, with Lake's permission."

"Of course, John," Lake told him.

"Well, everyone," John began, "we've been through a lot this summer. Funeral and fights. Broken hearts and broken friendships. Looking to the future we have the race in a few weeks and then Brandy and McKenzie's wedding. So as Lake accurately said that Easter morning, 'Life is hard, but God is good, and the best is yet to come."

"Jesus knew life was hard. He was known as an illegitimate child. He was single. To be single at that time one was considered less than a man. During his ministry people thought he was crazy, even his family. Some thought he was demon-possessed.

"When he needed his friends the most, at Gethsemane, they slept while he fought to get his flesh under control. Remember, he asked that the cup to be taken from him. After several times of prayer, he submitted to the will of his Father.

"Judas betrayed him. Peter denied him. Later that night, he was falsely accused during an illegal trial and later murdered. He knew life was hard and he experienced the worst of mankind.

"But he knew God was good. He knew the promises of God the Father. He knew he would rise again and be seated at the right hand of God. And he did it for us! That's why we celebrate his resurrection.

"We know God is good. We know the promises of God. Because of Jesus's death and resurrection, we now have hope. Because God is good, he provided Jesus, the sacrificial lamb, to pay the ransom for us.

"And yes! The best is yet to come! Because of his resurrection we now have hope! We'll live in eternity serving our Father. All tears will be gone! No more sin! No more death! We know because of Jesus's death and resurrection, we will rise again. Because of him, we will see our loved ones again. Because of him, we live.

"Life is hard, sometimes so very hard. But our Father is so loving and so good. And for those that believe in Yahshua, the best is yet to come."

"Thank you, John," Lake said as everyone clapped. "Brisk. You said you have something to say?"

"Well," she began, "you are not going to believe this, Lake, but my father read your Appalachian Trail Psalms and he was touched by what you wrote. He said, perhaps, you might not be such a crazy bohemian as he thought. He said you are certainly an unconventional Christian but a Christian indeed. He especially loved your psalm for the letter X, which you actually used the word *extravagant*."

"Really?" Lake asked surprised.

"What's *bohemian*?" Llewellyn asked.

"What are your Appalachian Trail Psalms?" Lydia asked.

As Lake continued managing the fire, he answered them. "I am not sure what *bohemian* means, but I can tell you about the trail psalms I wrote. I was in New Hampshire on the AT when, Jan, a dear, sweet saint wrote me a letter. She said she felt impressed to tell me I should write a psalm beginning with each letter of the alphabet. So I was obedient and wrote each psalm when I felt inspired as I hiked through New Hampshire and Maine on my way to Mt. Katahdin. I didn't have a word starting with an X, but I decided the word *extravagant* would be a perfect substitute."

As the darkness slowly enveloped the forest, Brisk read Lake's psalm. "Lake wrote this from home after finishing the Appalachian Trail. It's called 'Extravagant.' Your providence has been extravagant! Against the odds you have permitted me to trek so far and yet return home so safe. My Appalachian venture was not as a prodigal son but as an exploring disciple, seeking you and seeking you early when it is written that I will find you.

"The extravagance of your artistry was on display wherever my eyes chose to glance. During the lonely first nights when I questioned my decision, you cloaked me with your extravagant peace. On frosty hilltops, I was charmed by the extravagant displays you presented in the heavens. Within the wilds, I journeyed and slept safely because of your extravagant protection. As the distance and the days shortened, your extravagant attentiveness to this weary soul preserved me. Who am I to see and soak in all you have created? You have granted my heart's desires. Though my heart twisted with many stirring memories and emotions and the tears wrung out, you gently eased my heart's pains and allowed me to understand what I was experiencing: Extravagant love, only given by an extravagant God, you. Oh, let this warrior-in-waiting give birth to an extravagant devotion to you.

"Oh, beautiful Father, how can I thank you for your extravagant providence? How?"

"That was beautiful, Lake," John told him. "You spoke from your heart as you frequently do. Thank you for that."

"Um, you're welcome, John," Lake told him. "Now, everyone one. Grab a mountain pie maker and let's start making mountain pie pizzas."

Lake gave a demonstration on how to make a mountain pie. Some were successful, and some were not. But everyone was laughing and talking in sweet fellowship.

Night had fallen and clouds had ventured in. Except for the fire it was completely dark. The light from the flames lit up the camp as well as the front of the Treehouse. Crickets were singing but competing in vain with the katydids. A warm breeze pushed through the hilltop.

One by one, without instruction, each band member began playing their instruments. Brisk played the clarinet, Parker the saxophone, Brandy the violin, Lawrence acoustic guitar, and Zachariah on bass guitar. There were no drums at the Treehouse so Kenzie joined Lake, John, Llewellyn, and Lydia by the fire.

The music echoed through the woods. Their voices seemed almost heavenly as everyone sang praises to the Lord. When the third song began, Lake instructed everyone that it was to be a cappella. Their voices of heavenly praise were accented by the katydid and the crickets. A wilderness concert of a few devoted friends devoted to the Lord.

When the song was finished, Lake whispered, "Continue worshiping the Lord. Also, listen to the forest. We can normally see his physical creativity. Now, we can listen to his creativity."

Lake silently walked to the Treehouse and climbed the ladder to the first floor. He unwrapped the tarp over an old piano he calls Geraldine and tossed it aside. He sat down at the piano and dropped his head. He whispered, "Father, let me play once again. Let me recover what was taken away. I believe this is what you want me to do tonight." Then, slowly, he touched the keys. As soon as everyone heard the piano they looked up at Lake.

"It's now or never," he whispered to Geraldine. Lake began painfully slow playing an old song he remembered. Then he stopped. For a whole minute, there was silence. Then he softly started playing again. Minute by minute, the tempo increased. He began pressing the keys more deliberately. After a few minutes, he was at the correct tempo and playing smoothly.

Everyone looked at Lake in amazement. Tears were running down his face. Kenzie, also in tears, said in astonishment. "He regained his musical ability. He forgave himself and the Lord restored him. Thank you, Father!"

As they stood in front of the Treehouse, they listened to the piano reverberate through the trees. Brisk began to play her clarinet. A minute later, Brandy's violin joined in. After another minute passed, Parker began to play his saxophone. Zachariah and Lawrence joined the woodland orchestra.

After playing the song three times, Lake shouted, "Sing Hosanna." Everyone joined in repeating Hosanna to the music. The music and the voices were perfect synchronization.

Just before finishing the last stanza a heavy rain started. Everyone rushed under the treehouse. Lake quickly covered Geradine and slide down the ladder. He stood out by the drowning fire and signaled everyone to join him in the rain.

As they stood next to Lake, he prayed, "Lord, rain on us! Reign in us. Soak us with your love!" He raised his armed to heaven and continually thank the Lord.

"Lord. You are so beautiful!" John prayed.

"Blessed be your name, Lord God," Lawrence whispered.

As the shower eased Lake looked at everyone. He said, "You all are smiling. Because we are praising him in his wilderness. We are seeing his creation, and we are listening to his creation, we are feeling his creation and we are smelling his creation."

"Wow, Lake. What special night," Llewellyn told him. "I never experienced worship like that."

"Me neither," Lake replied. "We came to seek him, and he provided all the props."

"And he restores," Kenzie reminded Lake.

"I don't think I can comprehend that yet, Kenzie. It is too wonderful!"

"Listen!" Brandy told the others.

Parker was playing a beautiful saxophone solo from the top of the Treehouse. While everyone was listening, Lydia said, "Look!" and pointed to the sky. A waning gibbous moon peeped through an opening in the clouds.

As Parker continued his solo everyone pondered the evening in their hearts. The fire was almost out, and the rain had slowed.

"I don't want this night to end, Lake," Brisk told him. "I don't want the music to end. Listen to Parker play his heart out on top of the Treehouse."

"I don't want it to end either," Lawrence added. "This night is so beautiful. Blessed be the name of the God of Abraham, Isaac, and Jacob."

"You've come a long way in your walk with the Lord, Lawrence," Lake told him. "You all have. And I agree. I don't want the night to end either. But you know, someday our time with the Lord will never end."

Kenzie said, "When you see the moon, Lake, you believe it is the Lord saying he is with you."

"He is with us all tonight. He is with us all," Lake softly said while staring at the moon. "His love is everlasting. His love is extravagant."

13

Race Day

The alarm went off at 3:30 a.m., and Lake quickly turned it off. "What was I thinking?" he said out loud.

"What are you talking about, Lake?" Kenzie moaned.

"A hundred-mile race! What was I thinking!" Lake replied and then yawned.

"Well, in twenty-four hours or so, it will all be over and we'll celebrate and then sleep for a week."

"Go back to sleep, Kenzie. Your relay wave doesn't start until eight."

"Oh no, big bro…hey, I'm a poet!"

"No comment."

"As I was saying, big bro, I want to see you and Llewellyn start. Everyone does."

"Coffee's on. I'm getting a shower. Oh. What was I thinking?"

As Lake was getting ready someone knocked on the motel room door. Kenzie looked out the peephole and then opened the door. "Llewellyn! Come on in. What's up?"

"I wanted to see if Lake had any strategies for the race that I didn't know."

"He's in the shower and will be right out."

Another knock on the door. Kenzie looked out the peephole and opened the door. "Brisk! Good morning. What's up?"

"Good morning. I wanted to watch Lake get ready for the race. Hi, Llewellyn."

"Good morning, Brisk."

Lake walked out of the bathroom and a bit startled others were in the room. "Well, I'm glad I at least had my running shorts on already! Good morning."

"They want to see you prep for the race," Kenzie told him.

"Well, Llewellyn, you probably know everything, you're an ultra-runner."

"Yeah, but I wanted to know if you did anything special for your feet."

"This is what I do," Lake said a sat on the bed and lifted his feet onto the mattress.

"They are the ugliest feet I've ever seen!" Kenzie teased.

"As I was saying, I use Vaseline on my feet. First, I put a Band-Aid on the spot or two I know I usually get a blister. Then I rub Vaseline all around the toes, like this, to prevent friction there. Then just slide the socks on. I usually repeat this once or twice during the race. Sometimes I get to a tired state and don't care anymore. I also use the Body Glide on the heavy equipment and under my arms where the chest muscles and arms rub."

"What do you mean 'heavy equipment'?" Kenzie asked.

Lake looked at Kenzie as Brisk, and Llewellyn started laughing.

"Oh! Oh! Never mind. Sorry!" Kenzie replied, red-faced.

"Need sunscreen and ChapStick. Usually at an aid station they'll have disposable wipes. Use that to get any salt from the sweat off your body. That causes friction. If you see a creek, jump in.

Just before the race, I smear Aspercreme on my legs. Good to get that in before the pain actually starts.

"I don't carry a lot because just about everything is available at the aid stations. Aspirins, Pepto Bismol, Imodium ID."

"What do you need all that for?" Kenzie asked.

"Aspirin for the headache, Pepto to keep it down, Imodium to keep it in."

"Wow, and you guys run this for fun?" Brisk wondered while shaking her head.

"It is fun," Llewellyn told her. "You got to try it someday."

"If you can, switch running shorts around halfway," Lake continued. "They get sweaty and uriney. Sorry. Both can irritate your skin. Change your shirt or rinse it out. Also, about halfway, switch your running shoes to a slightly larger pair if and only if you feel any discomfort. As your feet swell a larger shoe may relieve any discomfort. But if all is working well, leave it be. Maybe change your socks.

"I'm getting my headlamp and jacket at aid station twelve. That will be between 6:00 p.m. and 8:00 p.m. I don't want to get stuck without a headlamp in the dark or a jacket. After sixty miles, the body is tired and even a little bit of coldness can shut you down. That's what happened to me last year.

"Don't start out with your headlamp. The moon's out, and it will be light soon. No use carrying it five miles to the first checkpoint."

"It's four twenty. We got to be at the starting line at four forty-five. You set, Llewellyn?"

"Yeah, we're on the same track. Let me put the Vaseline on my toes first."

"Go ahead. Kenzie and Brisk, will you guys be all right?"

"Stop worrying! We'll be fine," Brisk told him.

"I know, but I worry. Until we all cross that finish line I won't rest!"

"I'm ready Lake," Llewellyn told him.

"Okay. Oh, my nerves!"

"You okay, Lake?" Brisk asked him.

"He'll be fine, Brisk," Kenzie told her. "He's a grumpy bear until the race starts, then he'll relax and be in his natural state."

"I think that's a correct description of my prerace jitters. Brisk, will you get picture of the three Nidhatak brothers?" Lake asked as he handed her the camera.

"Sure. Get closer together. That's good," she said as she snapped the picture.

"Kenzie will be the next Nidhatak ultra runner," Llewellyn said with a smile.

"No, I think you Nuthataks are enough for this family," he replied, laughing. "Nuthataks, get it?"

"Everyone should be ready to see you guys off," Brisk said.

"They won't be up this early," Lake replied.

Just then, a knock on the door. Kenzie looked out the peephole and then opened up the door. "Hey, what's up?" he asked.

Benjamin, Lydia, Brandy, Zachariah, Parker, and Lawrence came into the room. They were excited about seeing Lake and Llewellyn start their one hundred miles.

Lake stood up and everyone quieted down. "Hey! We have a long hard exciting day ahead of us," he began. "We worked hard to get here. Let's do our best. As you all know, it's been a hard year. We've lost friendships. We lost family. We lost church leadership. We lost our way, at least I did. But God has restored us. We now have new family. We now have new friends. We now have new church leadership. We have found our way again.

"I'm proud of all of you attempting this race. I think a stronger bond will grow between us.

"As you, the Judah Lions, run the relay, pray for Llewellyn and me. As Llewellyn and I run the one hundred miles, we will pray for you, the Judah Lions.

"I calculate the Judah Lions will finish between 10:00 p.m. and midnight tonight. You'll start at 8:00 a.m., so that's fourteen to sixteen hours. Llewellyn and I expect to finish between five and seven tomorrow morning. That's twenty-four to twenty-six hours. The course has over eighteen thousand feet of elevation gain, which will slow us down.

"Please get plenty of sleep as you wait for you turn to run the relay. Drive safe. Eat and drink. The earlier you get done, the sooner you can rest, eat, and celebrate.

"Let's pray. Father, thank you for all this coming together. It's not about where we place in the race but how we commit ourselves and how we complete the race. I pray for safety for all the relay teams and all the ultras. I pray for Llewellyn as an ultra-runner. Make his dream of finishing a hundred-miler come true. I pray for the Judah Lions safety and relaxation for those waiting their turn to run, especially for those preparing to run their second relay. May we bless you somehow during this race. In the name of Yahshua. Amen. Let go. Three blocks to the starting line."

Lake and Llewellyn both ate some morning biscuits, a banana, and drank coffee as the group walked the short distance to the starting line. "Thanks for praying for me, Lake. This is a dream for you also. I pray your dream comes true in this race too."

"Thanks, new bro. I think it is going to be an awesome day today and tomorrow. Absolutely awesome."

As they waited for the announcement for the ultras to start, Lake talked to each member of the group individually. "Brisk, be careful," he said as he kissed her. "Brandy, you be careful too. Make sure Brisk behaves," and he kissed her on the forehead. "Parker! My little friend," Lake signed. "Please hold the noise down, will you?"

Parker signed back, "Thank you, Lake. I love you."

"Run well," Lake signed. "I want to see that big smile when I cross that finish line!"

Parker nodded his head and smile with affirmation.

"Zachariah, you got it in you. Press harder than you ever have. You are the key for this team. You are the most powerful for the hills. Do it."

"Thanks, Lake," he replied.

"Lawrence…lead. Be the leader today. They need you. You can do it."

"Lydia. Since you've already ran marathons, this is a piece of cake for you. The team looks to you for inspiration. Inspire them." He kissed her on the forehead.

"I will, Lake. I will," she promised.

"Benjamin. Benjamin. I'm so proud of you how you practiced and increased you speed and endurance. You are a speed asset for the Judah Lions. I'm excited for you. I expect a few sub-five-minute miles, right?"

"I'll try, Lake. You are the best coach. Thanks."

"Kenzie. Run and enjoy. We'll have a big celebration after we all rest up. You are the bestest brother. Thanks for running and thanks for letting me run this race."

"I don't think I had a choice about whether or not you could, Lake."

"No, but it sounded good!"

"Shut up and get up there, the ultras are lining up," Kenzie told Lake. Lake smiled and then Kenzie gave him a hug. "Be careful. Now get!" he yelled. "And Kick Llewellyn's ass!" After Lydia hugged Llewellyn, Kenzie gave him a hug also. "Go, big brother!" he yelled. "Kick Lake's ass."

Lake and Llewellyn laughed as placed their running packs on and walked to the finish line. The moon was still high in the western sky. The lights at the starting line lit up the two hundred ultra-runners getting ready to start. Lake and Llewellyn looked back one last time at the Judah Lions and waved.

"Ready, set, go!" The race began at precisely 5:00 a.m. The runners began slowly, preserving energy that they'll need for the day. Pounding of feet was all that could be heard and headlights pointing and turning in all directions was all that could be seen as the runners disappeared into the distance.

The Judah Lions quietly walked back to the motel for an hour or two more of sleep.

The ultra-runners proceeded down the dark road for several miles as the eastern sky grew brighter. Lake and Llewellyn talked together as they ran along the country road. At five thirty, the runners turn off the road and began walking up a trail having a 1,500-foot ascent. As they crested the ridge, the sun began shining on the runners, a big orange ball soon appeared.

"Okay, Llewellyn, we need to pass some of these walkers," Lake suggested.

"Yeah, this is too slow for me. We need to take it easy, but this is crazy," he replied.

"On your left!" Lake yelled.

"On your left," Llewellyn yelled.

They began to pass some runners. Other joined Lake and Llewellyn and followed behind them.

"I love this!" Lake yelled. They began descending and soon were at the first-aid station.

"Check it out!" one of the runners shouted.

"Welcome to aid station 1. We have eggs, sausage, pancakes, and juice. What do you need?" one of the volunteers asked the runners coming in.

Lake got a bagel with egg while Llewellyn got a bagel with sausage. "Wow, this is good! Thank you," Llewellyn told the volunteers.

"Yeah, thanks," Lake told them.

They began running down the road alongside a slow flowing river. "Check it out, Lake! Kayakers," Llewellyn point out.

"In a few hours, I hope to be jumping in there with them," Lake replied. "Too early now."

The morning was cool and pleasant. The runners went over several ridges, through several state parks, and more aid stations. The afternoon sun was getting hot and the aid stations encouraged the runners to drink plenty of liquids.

Lake's cell phone rang at 2:00 p.m. "Hello, Kenzie, how's the team doing? Good. Llewellyn and I are doing fine. The heat is getting to me a bit, but I'm looking for some place to jump in shortly. Hi, Brisk, how are you feeling? Good. Everyone having a good time? Great. Okay. Call me at six. Bye."

"Their doing great, Llewellyn. They said they are having the time of their lives."

"Hey, Lake. There's a creek and a swimming hole. Let's go!"

They ran down the road's embankment and took off their running shoes and socks. Both dived into the water. Lake came up from under the water. "Oh! That feels good. I hate that salt all over me."

"I never thought about jumping into a creek while running. It is refreshing," Llewellyn told Lake.

They both got out and placed their socks and shoes back on. "Let's go!" Lake yelled.

Lake and Llewellyn both came into aid station 12 just before 4:00 p.m., mile 50. The volunteers were quick to ask what they needed and to provide any assistance. Both runners retrieved their gear sent to this checkpoint for the run in the dark. A jacket, a headlamp, replacement socks, and running shoes. They ate cookies and a sandwich. As they were leaving, Lake said he didn't feel well. One of the volunteers was just about to eat a sandwich for herself. Lake said, "What's this barrel for?"

The volunteer said, "Trash." Lake thanked her and then placed his head into the barrel and threw up. The volunteer placed her sandwich back into the plastic bag she had.

"I'm sorry," Lake said.

"You okay, Lake?" Llewellyn asked.

"Oh, I feel great now. The typical ultra-run puke!"

"Yeah, my times coming shortly, I can feel it!"

"Our stomach is like a washing machine. After eleven hours, it's a mess! All that thrashing around."

Lake's cell phone rang. "Hey," he answered. "Good. Just leaving aid station 12, mile 50. Glad to hear everyone is doing so well. I don't know how we missed one of you guys running by. Getting tired on this end. Okay, see you then."

"They should finish a little after dark. Zachariah is running now and then Benjamin picks it up. They must have passed us by when we were swimming!"

"Yeah, they are doing great," Llewellyn agreed.

Lake and Llewellyn were on a ridgeline as the sun began to set. Lake said, "Let's pray." He knelt down facing the sun. Then Llewellyn knelt down. "Father, no sunset is ever the same. Thank you for showing us this one. I pray for all the runners to finish. I pray for the Judah Lions. I pray we safely make it through the night. In Jesus's name. Amen."

"Amen."

"Look, Llewellyn, the sunset is so beautiful. We have been running from sunrise to sunset. And it's been great. I didn't expect us to run this far together but we did. This is the bestest run yet."

"Yeah, Lake. I didn't expect to run together either but we seem to have the same pace. But now the difficult part: the night, the cold, the fatigue. I'm yawning already!"

"Yes! But we'll be watching and waiting for that glorious sunrise! Then we'll take it in! We'll finish the race that is set before us!"

"I'll walk in if I have to!"

"I'll crawl in if I have to! Quitting is not an option! Death is."

"I don't know if I'll go that far, Lake!"

"Hey, Llewellyn, I hear runners up ahead. Let's zero our radar in on them and pass them by!"

"Yeah! You make running fun! Even after fifty miles!"

"Let's go!" They took off running and passed several walking runners strolling down a beautiful grass road as dusk settled in. "Hey," Lake yelled. "Run with us!"

"Thanks, but we're taking a break. Sharp Top is just up a way. Save your strength!" one of the runners replied. Another one joined Lake and Llewellyn as they passed by and continued with them on the ascent up Sharp Top Mountain.

"This would be easy running one hundred miles if it weren't for the hills. Why do they do make ultra-running so hard?" Lake asked.

"Because anyone who runs one hundred miles is crazy so they put in the hills to make us insane."

"I think you're right. Headlight is now on!"

"Headlight on."

A few miles later, Lake stopped suddenly. "Look behind us!"

"Wow!" Llewellyn responded. "The full moon is so beautiful!"

"Yes!" Lake said while pointing to the moon. "I always think God is smiling on me when I see the moon. Then I know all will be all right. Hey, here comes somebody fast. Must be another relay runner."

"Is that you, Nuthataks?"

"Kenzie, is that you?" Lake asked. "Why are you here?"

"Yeah, it's me! Oh, man! Brisk dropped me off at the last aid station and will pick me up at the next. I just wanted to see my bros! This has been an awesome day! We are having the greatest time!" Kenzie told them.

"I'm glad to hear it, little bro. Hey, did you see that moon? God is smiling on us tonight!"

"Lake, he's always smiling on us."

"I know but the moon makes it extra special."

"It sure does, Lake. How are you doing, Llewellyn?"

"Great! We are over halfway!"

"Well, brothers, it's been nice chit chatting, but I gotta go!"

"Let's pray."

"I don't have time to pray, Lake. I have to meet Brisk at the next aid station!"

Lake grabbed Kenzie and Llewellyn joined them, all three headlamps facing each other. "Bless you, Kenzie. Now get!"

"Fine! Bye. You old guys are too slow for me!"

"Double fine," Lake replied.

"Triple fine?" Llewellyn carefully added.

"Be careful, big bros! See you at the finish line!" Kenzie yelled as his headlamp disappeared down the trail and into the woods.

"Kenzie's cool, Lake. Lake? You all right?"

"Yeah. Seeing my little brother disappearing into the dark, I worry about him. Now I have the ultra-cry!"

"You get that too? I never have been able to figure it out. What causes it?"

"Oh, I think it's when the flesh is broken and you are running, kind of, with your spirit. That's why the ultra-cry is a happy cry. We don't know what's happening. We cry and are happy! But seeing Kenzie run by pushed me into it a little early. Usually, it's not until I know I'm going to make it."

"The ultra-cry. Haha. It's a running phenomenon."

The running continued overnight. At one thirty, Lake and Llewellyn came into aid station 15. Christmas lights were hanging in the trees and on the railing that crossed a small stream. A bond fire was going near the food table.

"How are you guys doing?"

"We're good," Llewellyn answered.

"Well, we have to weigh you now to make sure you are keeping your weight up."

"Okay," Llewellyn answered as he stepped onto the scale.

"You lost a few pounds, which is normal. You should be fine."

Lake stepped onto the scales. "Lakeland, you lost a few also. Okay, both of you are good to go. Get something warm to eat. Take a bag of food. It's a long walk up the next hill."

Lake and Llewellyn thanked the volunteers and slowly walked into the woods. They ascended the next ridge and had a four-mile easy run to aid station 16. After eating a little and having their running packs filled with water, they headed out.

Lake saw a runner sitting in a chair wrapped up in a blanket. He went over and briefly talked to him. Llewellyn was surprised to see Lake pull the guy out of his chair. They were laughing as Lake encouraged him and physically pushed him down the trail. Then Lake walked back to retrieve his gear.

"Llewellyn. This is where I dropped out last year. I sat down too long, and it was so cold. It was like my body was shutting down. I was so disappointed in myself."

"Lake! You did seventy-six miles! That's an accomplishment. You should be proud."

"I don't want to be proud. I want to finish whatever race he sets before me. I failed last year. That's the only race I never finished."

"So! I think it's great you came back again this year."

"Well, God is good. And I know it will be doubly sweet to cross that finish line this year. Nothing is going to stop me. Nothing."

At 2:15 a.m., Lake's cell phone rang. "Yes, brother? Sorry, no cell service for a while. A few hours ago? Wow! You all did great! Better than expected. Now get back to the motel and get some sleep. Call me when you get up. I'm proud of all of you. Here's Llewellyn."

"Hey, Kenzie. Great job. Congrats to all! Yeah, please. Hi, Lydia. How you feeling? Good. Good. Get some sleep. Bye."

"They did great, Llewellyn. Twenty-fifth out of 110 relay teams. Wait until next year! Now they know what the course is like, they'll be back with a top 10 placing next year wait and see!"

Lake and Llewellyn continued running in the cool morning hours assisted by the moonlight.

"It's 3:45 a.m. We'll make it by six, seven, maybe eight. We're doing good, Lake."

"Haha! I bet the first-place winner is done, showered, and sleeping right now!"

"Yeah, I'm sure. But we're still having fun."

"Yes, we are. Never again! Never again!"

"Lake, Kenzie told me you'll say that and that you always say that during and after an ultra."

"Well, I think I mean it this time! I'm retiring from ultra-running!"

"We'll see!"

At 5:00 a.m., Lake and Llewellyn came into another aid station. This one had the forest decorated with Japanese lanterns. The volunteers were tired but more than generous with their hospitality. "Breakfast, guys?"

"Yes, please. It's been twenty-four hours of running. We're hungry."

"First, we have to weigh you." Lake got onto the scales first. "You're fine," the volunteer said.

When Llewellyn went onto the scale, she said, "Llewellyn Nidhatak, you got to stay until you can get some weight back on. Just two pounds will put you back into your safe zone."

"I'll wait for you, Llewellyn. Should only take twenty minutes or so."

"No, Lake. Go!"

"But I want to finish with you."

"I want to finish with you too. But if it doesn't happen it doesn't happen. I want you to finish without me delaying you. So go. Please. I'll try to catch up."

"Okay. I'll slow up some or something."

"No, Lake. Do your normal running. I'm drinking this Gatorade, and I won't be far behind you. As you told Kenzie, 'Get!'"

"Fine!"

"Double fine."

"Hey, it's been fun, Llewellyn. See you in a bit."

"See you shortly. Go!"

Lake walked into the woods glancing back to wave at Llewellyn. After walking a short distance, he began running painfully down the trail. The sun was beginning to lighten up the eastern sky.

He ran silently as the sun rose, granting another beautiful day. "Thank you, God, for making it through the night. I hope Llewellyn catches up to me. And thank you for the team finishing and doing so well. Another few hours, and I'll be done. Never again! That's not a promise God, I don't trust myself."

Every now and then, Lake would look behind him, hoping to see Llewellyn catching up. Then he turned and looked at the sun. "Another blessed beautiful day!"

14

Finish Line: I've Run the Race Placed before Me

At dawn, Lake came into the last checkpoint, exhausted but smiling. A female volunteer asked him what he needed. He replied, "I need a hug." She smiled and gave him a hug. "What do you need?" she asked as she pulled his pack off. "Water or Gatorade?"

"Just water, I'm Gatoraded out. Water will take me to the finish line," Lake quietly replied. "Oh, do you any Dr. Pepper?"

"Yes, we do," she replied as she retrieved a small can from the cooler. "Here you go."

"That's what they are going to have in heaven," Lake replied.

"Dr. Pepper?" she asked with a big smile.

After taking a long drink, Lake said, "Oh, yeah. Dr. Pepper and manna."

As she laughed, she asked, "Speaking of manna, do you want anything to eat?"

"Pizza?" he responded.

She reached across the picnic table and picked up two pieces of pizza and handed them to Lake. "Here you go. Anything else?"

"No, but a big thank-you." He said as he placed the two pieces of pizza together and made them into a sandwich. "I appreciate your kindness," he said as tears came to his eyes.

"You okay?" she asked as she hugged him.

"Yes, I'm happy right now. I'm going to finish, and… I just appreciate you and everyone out here helping. How's the rest of the course?"

"It's all road, the last few miles are slightly downhill through a beautiful canyon. A piece of cake for you now. You're going to make it. Congratulations," she told him.

"That's easy for you to say," he said with a smile. "Oh, my brother is coming in. He looks like me, his name is Llewellyn. Tell him to hurry up or his big brother is going to beat him."

"I'll give him your message," she said as she gave him another hug. He began to walk away backward, waving because he was too choked up to talk. She gave him thumbs up. Lake winked then turned and walked while he ate the pizza. When he finished eating, his cell phone rang. "Finally, cell service."

"Hey, Kenzie!" he answered. "You finished in under fourteen and a half hours? Congratulations, I knew you guys could do it! How is everyone? Did they have fun? Great! Just left the ninety-five-mile checkpoint, almost there, li'l bro, crank up the music! Nothing can stop me now. Where's Llewellyn? Then he shouldn't be too far behind me. He'll probably pass me by soon. Hey, isn't God good or what?! I'll call you before the last mile. God is so good, isn't he? I'm so proud of you, guys! I can't wait to see you all! Tell everyone, 'Great job.' See you when I get there, Kenzie. Bye."

As he walked, he prayed out loud, "God, thank you for the team finishing safely. Thank you for them to compete as a team. It's been a long day for them so bless them physically and spiritually. Thank you for everything falling in place so well today. Thank you for making it this far! Thank you, God! Llewellyn isn't far behind me. Let us both finish and glorify you. I pray for all the other runners too, bless those who didn't make it this year. It's painful to drop out, as I did last year. Comfort their hearts and draw them near to you. I pray for the ones who do finish that they realize you blessed them and allowed them to finish, not by their own means but everything is because of you. Let's take it in Lord. To the finish line!"

Lake told his legs, "Come on, start moving!" He began to run, his face expressing the pain in his legs. After a mile he caught up to another runner who was walking. "Come on, run with me. Only four miles."

"Thanks, dude," the other runner said. "I think I'll walk it in. You're looking good, keep going!"

Lake smiled and waved as he continued on the road.

A short time later, Lake passed the ninety-seven-mile marker. "Thank you, God. Thank you, God!" he said. "Three miles to go!" He stopped and knelt down. "God, thank you. Whatever you want. I don't know how, but I want to glorify you somehow today. Thank you."

"Oh, my legs!" he said as he stood up. "And my stomach, my head, my ankle, my arms, my feet, my everything. Never again, never again. Let's go. Three miles, you can do it, Lakeland Nidhatak." Before he started running, he took off his pack, checking to make sure the engagement ring was safe and sound. He didn't tell anyone about his plan, not even Kenzie. As he placed his pack on his back, he leaned forward to get some momentum and began the painful run to the finish line.

Lake was singing and praising God as he ran slowly, looking around, noticing the flowers and the mountains. He saw a deer on the road directly in his path. "If I were you, I'd get out of my way because this is a nonstop flight, deery! Scoot!" The deer's white tail flickered a few times, and then it disappeared in the woods. Lake smiled as he ran by where the deer had been, quickly looking into the woods, trying to see he could still see it. "Thank you, God, for creating all the woodland creatures!"

Llewellyn saw Lake up ahead and yelled his name. Lake turned around and, with a big smile, yelled, "Way to go new, bro! I've been looking for you!" Suddenly, when he turned back around, something hit Lake in the left side of his chest. As he swung around in pain, he fell down the road's embankment and into a small stream. Lake rolled over and leaned against the embankment.

"Lake!" Llewellyn yelled, not being able to see him. Lake didn't respond. He was trying to figure out what had happened. With his right hand, he reached over to the pain and felt something hard sticking out of his chest. "Oh, God, my God, why, why, why are you doing this to me? We're so close! It's always something! If it's not one thing, it's…" His eyes caught the writings his team placed on the back of his now torn race number:

Run the race that is set before you. Run, my brother.
Lawrence

Never, never quit!
Zachariah

Finish at all costs!
Brandy

Running is hard, but God is good. I want to see you cross that finish line!
Love, Brisk

Run, Little Wolf on the Lake, run. Dream! Run! Endure! Celebrate!
Love, you brother,
Mackenzie

See you at the finish line, new bro.
Llewellyn

See you at the finish line, my hero.
Love,
Parker'

Llewellyn slid down the bank. "What happened?" Lake pointed to his chest.

"Pray now. Pray how God will get me to the finish line so we might glorify him. We have to finish…at all costs."

"Oh, Lake, you have something sticking out of your chest. It looks like a broken-off arrow. We got to get help."

"First pray, right now…please."

"Um, okay. God, we need your help right now. Give us wisdom how to proceed. What do you want us to do? Jesus, help us. Oh, sweet Jesus, help us! Lake, we need help getting you out of here." He pulled out his cell phone from his pack. "No reception! No!" Llewellyn looked at the wounds. "I hope it didn't pierce any vital organs, Lake. Wait, I hear someone on the road." Llewellyn rushed up to the road and saw two runners. "Hey! I need some help," he yelled.

"What's wrong?"

"My brother's been hit by an arrow. I need help getting him up the bank."

The trio went down the embankment. One guy looked at Lake. "Hey, remember me? You're the guy who helped me out back at mile 76. I was going to quit until you pulled me out of the chair and made me run? You were right, after I got moving again, I was fine. I owe you, man."

"Yeah, I told you that you had it in you," Lake replied.

The other runner interjected, "I was walking way back and you coaxed me to run with you over Sharp Top Mountain. I'd be way back there if it wasn't for you. Now it's our turn to help you."

"How are we getting you out of here?"

"Well, we're all beat so be careful. I think we can angle up the bank. Someone can stay below me in case I fall. Someone to push me a little. We'll go up along those trees."

Slowly, the runners eased Lake up the embankment and onto the pavement.

"We made it, now we got to get help," Llewellyn said. He pulled out his cell phone again and exclaimed, "Still no reception! What gives?"

"We're in this canyon, no reception for about half a mile," one of the runners said.

"Sit down, Lake, until we get an ambulance."

"I'm finishing," Lake told him as he started walking.

"No, we're getting help. You can't finish."

"Yes, I can. Let's go. You can wait here if you want. I'm finishing with or without you. This is really going to mess up my finishing time."

Looking at the other runners, Lake told them, "Hey, you guys. Run in. I don't want to slow you up."

"I'm sticking with you," one runner said.

"So am I," said the other.

"Lake!" Llewellyn yelled.

"I'm not a quitter. I will finish. We will finish. Somehow, we'll glorify God. Look!" Lake pointed to the mile 98 marker.

"Two miles… Okay, let's do it!" Llewellyn reluctantly decided. "Sweet Jesus, help us!"

After a few minutes, Lake began to run.

"You are nuts, Lakeland Nidhatak! You are nuts!" Llewellyn yelled.

The runners were slowly advancing to the finish line in a horizontal row.

"What's your pain level Lake, on a scale of 1–10?"

"Eleven," Lake replied. "It's only when I breathe or move."

"Oh, man. Hey stop! Stop a minute! Your phone is ringing, Lake!" Llewellyn pulled Lake's phone out of his pack.

"It's Kenzie. Kenzie, listen! Do you see a cop or paramedics near you? Good! Lake's been hit by an arrow. Yes, as in bow and arrow! We need help fast! Between mile 98 and 99. What do you think? He's running! Go!"

"Help will be here in a few minutes, Lake."

"I don't need help here! I need it at the finish line! Do or die, I'm finishing! Let's go."

"That's what I'm afraid of!"

Lake walked a short distance then stopped. "Let's pray," he said. "Let's join hands. Jesus, it's all about you. Let it be all about you." Lake dropped hands and started walking. "Guys, get me to the finish line, please." Slowly, he started running.

At the finish line, Kenzie ran to the end of the bleachers and jumped off. He ran through the crowd to the first-aid station where the police, paramedics and ambulance were positioned. Seeing a policeman and a paramedic sitting together he yelled to them as he advanced. "Hey! Help!" They stood up as he neared." What's wrong?"

"My brother is one of the ultra-runners and he's been hit by a bow and arrow. He's between mile 98 and 99. Please help him!"

They both got on their radio and relayed the information to the others in their crew. With emergency lights and sirens, two police cars, the paramedics, and an ambulance drove through the crowd and onto the road. Kenzie suddenly realized he should have gone with one of the vehicles and ran in panic after them. Reaching the road, he stopped, knowing it was too late. He stood on the road, tears in his eyes watching the vehicles disappear. Then he thought, *Two miles, I can run out*. He began running up the road. After a short time, he heard a horn blowing behind him. It was one of the local television crews covering the race. Kenzie stood in the road blocking them. When the van stopped, he ran up to the driver. "My brother has been hit by an arrow, and he's running in. Let me go with you, please."

"Hop in." Kenzie opened the back door and got in.

"I'm Brian, one of the reporters. This is Beth, our producer, and we just heard someone got hit with an arrow, it's your brother?"

"Yeah, is that camera on?"

"Yes, do you mind?"

"I don't know! Just get me out there?"

"What's your name?"

"I'm Mackenzie Nidhatak. My brother is one of the ultra-runners, he's Lakeland Nidhatak."

"Can you tell us what happened?"

"At the last checkpoint, he was fine. My other brother Llewellyn was just behind him. Then I called wondering where they were and Llewellyn told me to get help because Lake got hit by an arrow. Llewellyn said, "Lake is still running!"

"Still running?" he said and looked at Beth. She nodded her head and got on her cell phone.

"What's going on?" Kenzie asked.

Going on mute, Brian quickly told Kenzie, "We're live locally, but she's going to see if this can be national. Okay, Mackenzie. Did you run today?"

While looking up the road, Kenzie answered, "Um, yeah. Lake organized some friends and me to run as a relay time. We finished some time ago."

"Hey, we're going national on the sports channel," Beth whispered.

"Wow, a busy day for you and your friends," Brian told Kenzie. "Sounds like Lake does a lot for you."

"He's the bestest brother in the world."

"What is your relay team's name?"

"Judah Lions."

"Where did you get that?"

"Jesus is the Lion of Judah, so if we are on his team, we are the Judah Lions."

"Oh," Brian replied startled.

"There he is! Stop! Let me out! Thank you for the ride!" Kenzie said as the van stopped and he ran toward Lake.

The paramedics were out of their vehicle, and the ambulance crew was removing a stretcher from the back. The police were the first to talk to Lake. The runners stopped when they saw all the commotion. "What happened and where?" one of the officers asked.

Llewellyn said, "Just before mile 98. There is an old truck parked there, it was just after that."

"I'll go check that truck out, maybe he's the hunter," one officer said and then left the scene.

"Okay, get on the stretcher," one of the paramedics said.

"Not yet," Lake told him.

"What do you mean? You got to go to the hospital. You're hurt bad, man."

Just then, Kenzie ran up to Lake with Brian and his TV crew behind him.

"Lake! Are you going to be all right?"

"Who are you?" the paramedic asked.

"I'm his brother, Kenzie."

"Well, tell you brother to get in the ambulance so we can take him the hospital. He's lost some blood."

"Big bro, why don't you listen to them and go get help."

"Lake, I'm Brian from Sports Central, you're live on TV. Why do you want to keep running?"

"Ah, because I'm not done yet, Brian? Or because I'm not a quitter? Or maybe, um, I want to bless God and bless my friends. Kenzie read what is written on my race number."

"Lake, please."

"Kenzie, we're here for this moment. I know it. Read."

"This is what we wrote on Lake's number while he was getting ready yesterday: 'Run the Race that is set before you, run, my brother, Lawrence. Never, never quit! Zachariah. Finish at all costs! Brandy. Running is hard, but God is good. I want to see you cross that finish line! Love, Brisk. Run, Little-wolf-on-the-Lake, run. Dream! Run! Endure! Celebrate! Love, you brother, Mackenzie. See you at the finish line, new bro, Llewellyn. See you at the finish line, my hero, love, Parker."

"Wow! That's pretty impressive, Lake," Brian told him. "Those are you friends at the end, the Judah Lions. And Kenzie your brother here?"

"Yes. Llewellyn is here with me. He ran the whole course also. He's my new brother. Plus, these two great guys helped me since I was hit."

"Your new brother?" he asked.

"We'll explain later," Llewellyn said.

"Lake, what are you going to do?" Kenzie asked.

"A little over a mile little brother, I have to do it. I have to finish. I will not quit. Grant me this one thing."

Kenzie looked at the paramedic. "Is he going to make it in?"

"I don't know. Maybe a puncture wound, hopefully not hitting any vital organs. Talk some sense into him, he's losing blood. What's your blood type, Lake, so we can have it ready?"

"B negative," Lake responded. "Okay, enough yip-yapping. I have to go!"

"Lake, are you allergic to anything," a nurse asked.

"Yes," he replied. "Bow and arrows." Everyone gave a cautious laugh.

"Let's go!" Lake told the runners.

"Are you really going to run it in, Lake?" Brian asked from behind the camera.

"You're not going anywhere. Get on the stretcher," a policeman told him.

"Look! A mountain lion," Lake yelled as he pointed into the woods. As everyone looked away, Lake took off running, followed by the runners, the TV crew, and watched by the startled emergency personnel.

"Hey, Kenzie, there's the road we ran up just after the race started yesterday, we must be a little more than a mile out from the start and finish line," Lake pointed out.

"Well, ain't that just fabulous. Now shut up and use your energy to get to the finish line."

"Boy, you're a bit snippy today, little one."

"Your one stubborn bastard, Lakeland Nidhatak!" Kenzie replied.

"I remember one stubborn bastard brother who wouldn't go to the hospital when his father beat the pulp out of him. Hey, there's mile 99. How sweet to my eyes. Thank you, Jesus."

"Lake, if you die, I'm going to kill you!" Kenzie yelled. "Llewellyn, why didn't you stop him?"

"Probably the same reason you're not able to stop him! One mile! Let's get him to the finish line then slap his ass on the stretcher!"

The group continued running down the forestry road with the TV crew alongside them and quietly being followed by the emergency vehicles. After a few quiet minutes the strap to the baton Lake was carrying around his neck came loose and the baton fell onto the roadway. Lake suddenly stopped as well as the other runners. The TV crew stopped and backed up to observe what happened. Brian asked, "What was that you dropped, Lake?"

"My baton fell off," he answered. "Will you get it, Kenzie, please?" he asked.

Kenzie picked up the baton and began to tie it back together around Lake's neck.

"Why do you have a baton?" Brian asked.

"I always carry it with me. I have etched on it Hebrews 3:13, which says, 'Remember the prisoners as if chained with them—those who are mistreated—since you yourselves are in the body also.' We are to remember our brothers and sisters who suffer for the sake of the gospel of Jesus. People in the USA don't realize the luxury we have with freedom of religion. But around the world, our Christian brothers and sisters are literally dying every day because they believe in Jesus. We need to stop sitting on the fence and commit to what we believe. We need to not be ashamed. Christians are not wimps! We can do all things, not in our own strength, but because he strengthens us. I also believe we must pass on the gospel to the next generation, like a baton. Oh, thank you, God, for this day! For allowing us to proceed this far. For allowing us to see your creativity in these beautiful mountains! You are God!"

"Okay, Pastor Nidhatak. Your baton is good to go for another one hundred miles," Kenzie told Lake.

"Hey, no one got out of the emergency vehicles. Guess they're going to allow you to finish," Brian said to the group.

"Let's put it in cruise," Llewellyn said as they started running.

A short time later, three police cruisers approached the group and stopped just a head of them.

"No, don't let them stop us now. Please, you guys, we got to make it in," Lake pleaded. "I can make it, I can make it. God help us." Lake looked at Kenzie then grabbed him by the arm. "Kenzie, I'm so tired. But I have to finish. Don't let them stop us."

"Lake! Look!" Kenzie shouted.

Out of the police cruisers stepped Lawrence, Lydia, Zachariah, Parker, Brisk, Brandy, Benjamin, and John, who was in his police uniform. They all ran up to Lake but didn't say a word as John instructed them. John looked intensely at Lake. Lake pleaded, "Don't stop me, John, please."

"First," John firmly began, "we're going to pray."

"John, please, please…"

"Then, we're running in with you." Lake dropped his head as everyone surrounded and laid hands on him as John prayed. "Father, as Lake always reminds us, it's all about you. You placed Lake here for this moment. Let us glorify you, in Jesus's name. Amen."

"That's our dad," Kenzie told Brian whose eyes got large when he said that.

"How'd you know we were out here?" Kenzie asked. "I just ran for help and didn't tell anyone."

"Oh, you were on those giant screens behind the stage. We saw everything," Brandy told them.

"All the people are quiet and watching. It's awesome," Zachariah said.

"Lake, oh, man. What are you doing?" Lawrence said very distraught over seeing Lake's wounds. "I'll help you in but never again! Do you know how much stress you put us through? I don't like seeing you hurting. What are you trying to prove?"

"I not trying to prove anything," he answered. "I just will not give up. I want to bless my sisters and brothers, and most importantly, Yahweh, creator of heaven and Earth."

"Brisk, come here," Lake asked. She walked slowly up to him.

"Lake, please get help. It doesn't look good."

"Brisk, trust me, please."

"I trust you. I don't want to lose you."

"Trust me," he said as he kissed her.

Parker signed to Lake, "I love you."

Lake signed back, "I love you more."

Parker smiled and shook his head no. He signed, "I love you more."

"You have less than half a mile, and you're running out of blood, let's go! Life Flight is waiting," John told Lake.

The three police cars turned around and led the runners in toward the finish line. The TV crew still remaining alongside the runners and the paramedics and ambulance brought up the rear.

A short time later, Zachariah asked, "Lake, can you do the cadence like when we run in the woods?"

"Are you nuts?" Lawrence shot back. "He has an arrow through him, plus he just ran ninety-nine and a half miles. Let him alone!"

"It's okay, Lawrence, Zachariah made a good suggestion, but I don't think I have the breath to do cadence."

Parker signed to Lake, "Can you recite one of your favorite scriptures?"

Lake smiled and then signed back, "As you wish."

"Everyone, repeat after me," Lake told them.

"The Lord reigns."

"The Lord reigns."

"Let the Earth be glad."

"Let the Earth be glad."

"Let the distant shores rejoice."

"Let the distant shores rejoice."

"Clouds and thick darkness surround him."

"Clouds and thick darkness surround him."

"His lightning lights up the world."

"His lightning lights up the world."

"Fire goes before him."

"Fire goes before him."

"And consumes…" Lake lost his balance and clung onto Llewellyn. Kenzie grabbed his other side.

"That's enough. Get the ambulance up here," John ordered on his radio.

Parker stood in front of Lake and began tapping him on his good shoulder. "What is it, Parker?" Lake asked, completely exhausted.

Parker signed, "The finish line! Look!"

"The finish line!" Lake said with delight. "I can taste it. Someone, get in my pack, please."

Kenzie opened the pack. "What?" he asked.

"The church flag, American flag, and the carrot."

"A carrot?" Brian asked. You carried a carrot a hundred miles?"

The church flag is for my God, the American flag for my country, and the carrot is for…" Tears came down his face.

"For his beloved dog Sheba," Kenzie told him. "She loved carrots. She died recently."

"She was my only friend," Lake said with a slight smile to agitate his friends.

"Oh, shut up!" Lawrence told him.

"With what I saw today, Lake, you've got a lot of friends," Brian told him.

"I know. They're the bestest. I am blessed," Lake replied.

Parker, jumping up and down and pointing, signed to Lake again, "The finish line!"

Lake saw the incentive and began running the best he could. With his right hand he held the flags and the carrot high as he neared the finish line. Kenzie ran on one side and Llewellyn on the other, balancing Lake and keeping him on a straight line. The rest of the band followed behind them.

The crowd was nearly silent as the runners approached. Just before the finish line a thunderous applause rang out. Lake collapsed into a chair waiting for him after crossing the finish line.

"You did it, Lake!" Lawrence shouted.

"You did it, Lake," Brisk said as she kissed him.

"We all did it. Llewellyn was right with me. He finished a hundred miles too. So did these guys who helped me in. What was my time?"

"Shut up! You finished. That's good enough," Kenzie told him.

"I'm not finished yet." As the paramedics prepared him for the life flight, he asked Brian to ask for quiet and then signaled for Brisk to come close. The paramedics lifted him onto a gurney. "Allow me to sit up," Lake asked, and they obliged.

"Brisk," he said, "will you marry me?"

"What?" she asked.

"Will you marry me?" he repeated. The crowd was quiet as most watched the proposal on the big-screen TVs.

"Yes!" she said, and the crowd went wild.

"Okay, get him in the life flight. We have room for two relatives."

As Lake was placed into the life flight, Kenzie and Brisk climbed aboard. The pilot powered up the helicopter, and they lifted off, heading south toward Thorndale. Lake's friends watched the helicopter disappear beyond the mountains.

"Benjamin, Llewellyn, Lydia, Brandy, Zachariah, Lawrence, and Parker, this is what I suggest," John began. "There is nothing you can do at the hospital, so I suggest you all get some rest. Go to the Eddy and get some sleep. Later, call everyone you can, and ask for prayer. Tell friends to come to the Eddy to lift Lake up to the Lord."

Parker began tapping John's hand and then simultaneously began pointing to the east and to the west. "What is it, Parker?" John asked.

Lawrence told John that one of Lake's favorite things is seeing the moonrise and the sunset at the same time. "Now we are seeing the moonset and the sunrise at the same time, and Lake is missing it!"

John laughed a little then told everyone, "He's flying at ten thousand feet. I'm sure he's seeing it, and if not, he's telling the pilot to turn the helicopter so that he can."

"Thanks, John," Lawrence told him. "We'll head to the Eddy. Please let us know anything you hear about Lake."

"I will. Drive carefully."

A police car pulled up to where John was standing. Trooper Bauer got out holding a plastic bag with a broken arrow in it. "John, this was found at the site where one of the runners that was with Lake said the incident occurred. There is fresh blood on it, so I am confident we have the correct arrow.

"And, John, there is a name on the arrow. Do you know this guy?"

John took the plastic bag and looked at the arrow. His demeanor changed, and he suddenly looked distressed. Then he read the name on the arrow aloud: "Justin Bentley."

About the Author

Lakeland Nidhatak grew up in the Appalachian Mountains of northern Pennsylvania. He is an accomplished long-distance runner, competing in over twenty ultra runs, including fifty miles, seventy miles, and one hundred miles. He also is an accomplished long-distance backpacker, having hiked the Pacific Crest Trail, the Continental Divide Trail, and completed the Appalachian Trail four times. One of his Appalachian Trail hikes was the central part of his hike on the unofficial Eastern Continental Trail from Key West, Florida, to Ravens Point, Newfoundland, Canada.

Lakeland has been a Christian since he was fifteen years old. He began his writing in junior high school and has many short stories and poems. While hiking the Appalachian Trail in 2008, he wrote his Appalachian Trail Psalms. *The Race* is his first attempt at writing a book.